WHALES

Published in Great Britain in 1997 by
Colin Baxter Photography Ltd,
Grantown-on-Spey,
PH26 3NA
Scotland
www.worldlifelibrary.co.uk

Text © Phil Clapham 1997
Illustration © Harriet Corbett 1997
All rights reserved
Reprinted in paperback 2001

A CIP Catalogue record for this book is available from the British Library

ISBN 1-84107-095-5

Photography copyright © 1997 by

Front cover © Flip Nicklin (Minden Pictures)
Back cover © Mark Carwardine (Innerspace Visions)
Page 1 © Brandon Cole (Norbert Wu)
Page 4 © Flip Nicklin (Minden Pictures)
Page 8 © Michael S Nolan (Innerspace Visions)
Page 11 © Flip Nicklin (Minden Pictures)
Page 12 © Paal Hermansen (NHPA)
Page 15 © Doug Perrine (Innerspace Visions)
Page 17 © Mark Ruth (Innerspace Visions)
Page 18 © Kennan Ward
Page 21 © François Gohier
Page 22 © François Gohier
Page 25 © Doc White (Planet Earth Pictures)
Page 27 © François Gohier
Page 28 © François Gohier
Page 31 © Tom Walker (Planet Earth Pictures)
Page 32 © François Gohier
Page 34 © Doug Perrine (Planet Earth Pictures)
Page 37 © Colin Baxter
Page 39 © Doug Perrine (Innerspace Visions)
Page 40 © François Gohier
Page 43 © Peter Howorth (Norbert Wu)

Page 44 © Peter Howorth (Norbert Wu)
Page 46 © Tui De Roy (Oxford Scientific Films)
Page 49 © François Gohier
Page 50 © Tui De Roy (Oxford Scientific Films)
Page 52 © Doug Allan (Oxford Scientific Films)
Page 55 © Doug Perrine (Planet Earth Pictures)
Page 56 © François Gohier
Page 58 © (top) Mark Carwardine (Still Pictures)
Page 58 © (bottom) Pieter Folkens (Planet Earth Pictures)
Page 60 © Bill Wood (NHPA)
Page 63 © Anthony Joyce (Planet Earth Pictures)
Page 64 © François Gohier
Page 67 © A.N.T. (NHPA)
Page 68 © François Gohier
Page 71 © T Kitchin & V Hirst (NHPA)
Page 72 © François Gohier
Page 75 © François Gohier
Page 77 © François Gohier
Page 78 © Bob Cranston (Norbert Wu)
Page 81 © James D Watt (Planet Earth Pictures)
Page 82 © Flip Nicklin (Minden Pictures)
Page 85 © Flip Nicklin (Minden Pictures)

Page 86 © François Gohier
Page 89 © François Gohier
Page 91 © Mark Conlin (Planet Earth Pictures)
Page 92 © François Gohier
Page 95 © Flip Nicklin (Minden Pictures)
Page 96 © Flip Nicklin (Minden Pictures)
Page 99 © François Gohier
Page 100 © Kennan Ward
Page 103 © Kim Westerskov (Oxford Scientific Films)
Page 105 © François Gohier
Page 106 © Ben Osborne (Oxford Scientific Films)
Page 109 © Morgan (Greenpeace)
Page 112 © Ben Osborne (Oxford Scientific Films)
Page 115 © Marty Snyderman (Innerspace Visions)
Page 116 © T Kitchin & V J Hurst (NHPA)
Page 120 © David Fleetham (Oxford Scientific Films)
Page 123 © François Gohier
Page 124 © François Gohier
Page 127 © François Gohier
Page 128 © François Gohier
Page 129 © François Gohier

Printed in Hong Kong

WHALES

Phil Clapham

Colin Baxter Photography, Grantown-on-Spey, Scotland

For Karen

There Leviathan,
Hugest of all living creatures, in the deep
Stretched like a promontory sleeps or swims,
And seems a moving land; and at his gills
Draws in, and at his breath spouts out a sea.
Milton: *Paradise Lost*

Contents

Fin Whale: 70 ft; 21 m

Northern Right Whale: 55 ft; 17 m

Gray Whale: 46 ft; 14 m

Sei Whale: 46 ft; 14 m

Bowhead Whale: 60 ft; 18 m

Minke Whale
26 ft; 8 m

Blue Whale: 85 ft; 26 m

Southern Right Whale: 55 ft; 17 m

Orca: 26 ft; 8 m

Bryde's Whale: 43 ft; 13 m

Sperm Whale: 50 ft; 15 m

Humpback Whale: 46 ft; 14 m

Introduction

whale, n. 1. A cetaceous mammal of fish-like form, especially one of the larger pelagic species, or a whalebone-whale.

Funk & Wagnall's *New Standard Dictionary* (1937)

In the Gulf of Maine off the east coast of the United States, there is a humpback whale that I and my colleagues have known for over twenty years. Her name (at least, our name for her) is Salt, so called because of a broad stripe of white on the leading edge of her dorsal fin. It looks as though someone once liberally sprinkled salt over her, which somehow stuck. Salt is a large female, the mother of at least seven sons and daughters. She is also the grandmother of at least one whale, though whether she is aware of this distinction isn't clear.

My mind hoards many fond memories of this most familiar of whales, garnered from the scores of occasions on which she and I crossed paths at sea. Among them are several comical images, and none more so than one drawn from a calm summer's day in 1985 when Salt and her latest calf, motivated by nothing more than simple curiosity, idly circled a small pleasure boat. The boat's two occupants, a man and a woman, scrambled desperately to the wheelhouse roof, which was as far as they could practically get from the water. There they stood, rigid and back to back, clutching the small mast and looking down in obvious terror on the two monsters that calmly swam round and round within a few feet of their boat. And there they remained for a full ten minutes, before Salt finally lost interest and shepherded her young daughter elsewhere.

This story, for all its humor, tells us much about how we still look at whales. Today, we know a good deal about these animals, and our image of them is no longer that common in the Middle Ages, when they possessed an almost supernatural quality in the minds of men. Yet, though our science has now largely demythologized whales, such is their presence that they retain the ability to inspire in human beings awe, wonder and even fear.

Whales are the largest animals on our planet. Cloaked in the mystery of the sea, they lead lives which are largely removed from the sight of humans, yet for centuries they have fascinated people all over the world with their size, grace and power. They have inspired books and poetry, stories and myths, and more than a handful of wildly exaggerated traveler's tales.

Our view of these most impressive of animals has undergone many changes over the centuries. As Arthur Koestler said, we can only add to knowledge, never subtract from it. Thus today, it is difficult for us to set aside all that we have learned about whales and to imagine how these vast and mysterious creatures would have appeared to our ancestors. Hundreds of years ago, what would have passed through the mind of a peasant fisherman, adrift in a small wooden boat, who suddenly found himself in terrifying proximity to an adult blue whale? Large beyond measure and possessed of unimaginable power, the creature must truly have seemed a monster of the deep. At least the two people terror-stricken by Salt and her calf knew that whales are corporeal beings rather than demons; the same cannot necessarily be said for superstitious men in ancient times.

A look at the etymology of our names for this animal is revealing. To the Greeks it was *ketos*, a word whose root means 'sea monster'. Our own English word *whale*, and all its relatives in Germanic and Norse languages (*wal*, *hval*, *hvaler* et cetera), probably derive from the word for wheel. This calls up an image of people standing on an ancient shoreline, gazing out to sea and straining their eyes to watch a distant whale surface, breathe and dive – for the latter action is characterized

The massive body of a southern right whale crashes through the surface in a powerful breach.

in all whales by a smooth rolling of the arched back, like a wheel turning in the water. The remoteness of this vision captures much of how whales must have been viewed for so long. They were creatures that made brief appearances in the lives of men, emerging from the darkness of the depths, and quickly returning to that same alien void.

Gradually, however, familiarity dispelled some of the mystery associated with whales, a change that was inevitably followed by a more adversarial relationship. Human hunting of whales is an ancient practice in some cultures, and was once attended by great ritual. The culture of many Inuit (Eskimo) peoples was so dependent upon marine mammal harvests that shamans devoted much ritual effort to ensuring the success of a whale hunt, and to respectfully propitiating the spirit of the whale after it had been killed. A rather similar practice occurs even today among whalers in Japan, who annually hold a 'funeral' for whales killed in the past year.

No such reverence attended the exploitation of whales by Europeans. Beginning with simple coastal fisheries for right whales in the 11th century, the expansion of whaling was subsequently fueled by the great explorations of the Renaissance. Eventually, virtually all of the whale's haunts and habits were exposed. By the time the 20th century came around, the industrial revolution had already set the stage for a mechanized slaughter that was unparalleled in the annals of wildlife exploitation, with some two million whales killed in the Southern Ocean alone.

As we emerge from this dark period, the future of some whales hangs in the balance. We cannot yet say that human beings have caused the extinction of any whale species, but we have come perilously close. Some populations of the northern right whale have virtually vanished, and the couple that remain number in the low hundreds. The same is true for bowhead whales in the eastern Arctic and the Okhotsk Sea, and for western gray whales.

But perhaps the most astonishing of all is the blue whale. That it is the largest animal ever to have lived in the four-billion-year history of our planet, a breathtaking creation of evolution, meant nothing to commercial whalers, who slaughtered blue whales by the hundred thousand. Today, most populations of blue whales are dangerously small, and only time will tell whether the species will recover from the devastation that it suffered at the hands of mankind.

With the decline of large-scale commercial whaling in the 1970s, a handful of biologists began to study living whales. Often identifying individuals from natural markings, they initiated long-term studies that have since blossomed and taught us much about the biology and behavior of these largest of all animals. Today, as a result, we know a good deal about some whales, although considerably less about others.

* * *

Whales is not intended as a field guide. There are many excellent works of that ilk, one of the best of which is referenced at the end of this book. Nor is it a comprehensive review of all cetaceans, which would be a major undertaking. Occasional mention is made of dolphins, porpoises and beaked whales, but these animals are not covered systematically. Rather, this book is offered as an introduction to the natural history of those most impressive and fascinating of all marine creatures, the great whales.

The killer whale or orca (which is not a great whale, merely a rather large dolphin), has been included by popular demand, on the basis that orcas, as well as being remarkable animals about which we know a great deal, are occasional predators of even the largest whales. Similarly, while all the other baleen whales make an appearance in this book, the pygmy right whale (whose scientific name is *Caperea marginata*) does not. This is essentially because we know very little about its biology and behavior. The pygmy right whale leads such a mysterious life in the cold waters of the Southern Ocean that sightings of this smallest of the baleen whales are exceedingly rare.

Overall, *Whales* is intended as an overview of what we do, and still don't, know about the creatures called whales — creatures which, for all our knowledge of them, remain in some ways as mysterious and as impressive as the great oceans in which they pass their lives.

The broad tail flukes of a sperm whale are raised in the air as the animal begins a dive. The whale will descend into lightless depths, perhaps as much as 2 miles (3.2 km) from the surface. The pattern of scalloping on the tail's trailing edge is used by scientists to identify individual sperm whales.

Origins

There is that leviathan, whom Thou hast made to play therein.
Psalms 104: 26

The Evolution of Whales

The sundry collection of aquatic animals that we know as whales, dolphins and porpoises are collectively referred to as cetaceans ('se-TAY-shuns'). The word derives from the ancient Greek word *ketos* (still in use today), meaning 'whale' or 'sea monster'. Long regarded as fish, cetaceans were officially classified as mammals in 1776 by the great Swedish naturalist Linnaeus, who stated with appropriate solemnity, 'I hereby separate the whales from the fish'. Like us, cetaceans breathe air, give birth to live young, and nurse those young with milk. The group encompasses a broad range of species that are found in all of the world's oceans, and even in a few of its major rivers.

Cetaceans range in size from the very small to the astonishingly large. At one end of the size scale is the tiny harbor porpoise, which is a mere 4 ft (1.2 m) long. At the other end is the blue whale, the largest animal that has ever lived, which can reach lengths exceeding 100 ft (30 m). Although seals, otters and a variety of other mammals spend much of their lives in the water, only cetaceans live a fully aquatic existence, never coming to land.

There have been cetaceans in the Earth's seas for a very long time, although they did not always appear quite as they do today. The broad outline of their evolutionary development from terrestrial mammals is quite well known, although inevitably the fossil record contains many gaps. Approximately 60 million years ago, shortly after the great extinction that claimed among its victims the dinosaurs, an unremarkable group of mammals known as condylarths existed by the water. These were rather small animals that were destined for great things: not only did they become the ancestors of all cetaceans, but also of the group of modern land mammals known as ungulates. This is apparent from various analyses, including some very recent genetic comparisons that demonstrate the close relationship between cetaceans and animals such as deer, sheep and hippos.

The condylarths lived out their lives on coasts or in river estuaries at the edge of the Tethys Sea, an ancient body of water that covered much of what is now central Asia before it was diminished and changed by great tectonic movements. For some reason, the condylarths began to spend some of their time in the water, probably to exploit new sources of food or to escape predation on land. While this move into an aquatic environment must have been advantageous, it presented the animals with many new problems that required evolutionary solutions. As a result, many adaptations began to occur in their morphology and physiology, some of which can be traced in transitional fossils. Over millions of years, the body took on a more streamlined shape and developed a powerful horizontal tail for easier movement through the water. The hind limbs eventually disappeared, while the forelimbs became modified into flippers. The nose gradually moved back from the tip of the animal's snout to the top of its head, making it easier to breathe without water entering the lungs. Fat layers were thickened to give insulation in cold water. The animals also evolved the ability to dive, and with it a whole suite of remarkable physiological changes.

When did the first true cetaceans appear? The earliest fossils of animals whose existence was completely aquatic date from approximately 45–50 million years ago. Known as archaeocetes ('ancient whales'), they encompassed a considerable diversity of species and

Killer whales are the highest predators in the marine ecosystem, and will sometimes kill even the largest whales.

included some very large animals. While none seem to have been the size of the blue or fin whales of today, it is clear that some reached considerable lengths: for example, an archaeocete known as Basilosaurus was more than 70 ft (21 m) long.

For reasons that are unclear, the last archaeocetes became extinct perhaps 25–30 million years ago. Nonetheless, from these most ancient of whales evolved the lineages that led to the two groups, or suborders, of modern cetaceans. One of these, the odontocetes (from the Latin, meaning 'toothed whales') today comprise the majority of species, including all of the dolphins and porpoises as well as the sperm whale and a rather odd group known as ziphiids, or beaked whales. As the name indicates, all of the odontocetes have teeth, although the number varies by species from one to many.

By contrast, members of the other suborder have no teeth at all. These are the mysticetes (also Latin, meaning 'moustached whales') or baleen whales. Instead of teeth, their mouths contain hundreds of hard plates of baleen that together act as a huge strainer, with which the whale sifts small prey from the surrounding water. Today, there are about a dozen species of baleen whales. They include all of the largest cetaceans except for two species: the sperm whale and an animal called Hyperoodon. The latter species, also known as the giant bottlenose whale, is poorly understood, but can reach lengths of more than 40 ft (13 m). We will meet the sperm whale later.

Modern cetaceans comprise about 79 species. We say 'about' for two reasons. First, there is disagreement about what constitutes a species. For example, we know from recent DNA studies that one of the large whales, the Bryde's whale, is not a single species but at least two and perhaps three. Similarly, the classification of the familiar bottlenose dolphin is a topic of much debate, with some scientists claiming not only that there are two species, but that these belong in separate genera (the next level of taxonomic classification).

Second, it is not unlikely that undiscovered species of cetaceans still roam the world's oceans. Although many whales and dolphins are easy to find, some are not. Indeed, one described species

(Longman's beaked whale, *Mesoplodon pacificus*) has never been observed alive in the wild, and is known to exist only because of stranded specimens! We suspect that there may be more species of beaked whales than are currently recognized. Beaked whales live in deep water often far from land, and many seem to have a very secretive lifestyle. It was as recently as 1991 that the latest species, named *Mesoplodon peruvianus*, was described by science.

The species of whales that we recognize today have existed for various lengths of time. The oldest seems to be the sperm whale, which evolved well over 20 million years ago. The beaked whales are also an ancient group. Baleen whales have been around in one form or another for about 40 million years, but all of the current species seem to be much younger than this. However, it is quite possible that some of the modern species evolved earlier, and that we have simply not yet found fossilized remains from this period.

Cetacean Classification

Every described species on Earth has a scientific name that is unique to that species. All species are classified hierarchically in a series of categories according to the degree to which they share evolutionary descent. Thus, all animals, including whales, are grouped in the 'kingdom' Animalia, which is separate from the kingdom that includes (for example) plants. Each kingdom is divided into a series of 'phyla'. Cetaceans are one of numerous groups belonging to the phylum Chordata, which includes all animals that have (at some stage of their development) a notochord (a long flexible rod of cells that forms the supporting axis of the body). Chordates encompass the 'subphylum' Vertebrata, or vertebrates. Within this category are numerous 'classes', one of which is Mammalia, or mammals. Below the category of class comes that of 'order', and here cetaceans are grouped together in their own exclusive order, Cetacea.

The order Cetacea is further subdivided into three 'suborders': odontocetes (toothed whales), mysticetes (baleen whales), and the extinct archaeocetes. Each suborder contains various 'families', which

A southern right whale glides by, showing its massive head and arched jawline. The white areas on the head
are called callosities. Naturally dark, each callosity is given its light coloring by huge colonies of whale lice. The pattern
of callosities is unique to each individual right whale.

themselves comprise one or more 'genera' (the plural of 'genus'). And within each genus is one or more species. The scientific name of any living thing consists of two parts, being the names of the genus and of the species. The blue whale, for example, is *Balaenoptera musculus*, where *Balaenoptera* is the genus and *musculus* the species. The closely related fin whale, being in the same genus, is *Balaenoptera physalus*.

How do the species we will meet in this book fall into this scheme? Sperm and killer whales are of course both toothed whales, in the suborder Odontoceti. The sperm whale is assigned to the family Physeteridae, which also includes the pygmy and dwarf sperm whales. The killer whale is grouped with the family Delphinidae, the oceanic dolphins, for it is actually a large dolphin.

The baleen whales (the suborder Mysticeti) comprise four families. The largest family is the Balaenopteridae, also known as the 'rorquals', from a Danish word meaning 'tubed' or 'pleated' whale, a reference to the pleats found on the underside of all rorquals. This family includes two genera and six species (the blue, fin, sei, Bryde's, minke and humpback whale). The family Balaenidae is the right whales (northern right, southern right, and bowhead). The gray whale is alone in its own family, Eschrichtiidae. The fourth family, Neobalaenidae, includes just the pygmy right whale, which is not included in this book.

It is important to realize that scientific classification is an imperfect system which sometimes requires revision. Broadly speaking, all taxonomy is based upon the theory that species which are closely related (that is, those which shared a common ancestor in the very recent past) will share a greater proportion of morphological or genetic 'characters' than those whose ancestors diverged further back in evolutionary history. In practice, however, this exercise requires us to make certain subjective judgements, and to understand a good deal more about the processes of morphological and molecular evolution than we often do. For example, since mutations (a simple change in

the DNA at one base, or 'site') will occur in certain genes over long periods of time, the degree to which different species share such mutations is taken as an indication of how recently those species shared a common ancestor. But many questions must be answered for us to have confidence in such assessments. Do the mutations occur at a constant rate over millions of years? Do they occur at different rates in different species? Do they occur more frequently in certain parts of the gene? What if a single site in the gene has been subject to two or more mutations (in which case we will see only the most recent one)? Morphological analyses have similar problems. For example, if two species share a common morphological feature, is this an indication of shared ancestry, or does it mean that both species independently evolved this feature? The result of all this uncertainty is that debates about classification are a constant feature of taxonomy.

Whales are no exception. A recent DNA analysis by Dr Michel Milinkovitch suggested that sperm whales were actually more closely related to baleen whales than to other toothed whales. However, this particular theory is hotly contested by most morphologists, and other geneticists have produced different molecular data to 'confirm' that sperm whales are indeed odontocetes. This debate nicely exemplifies the problems with all such forms of analysis, and highlights the basic problem that we know too little about the mechanisms of molecular and morphological evolution to state many things with certainty.

Whatever the precise mechanisms involved, the evolution of all the cetaceans was accompanied by a series of dramatic changes in morphology and physiology. Indeed, modern cetaceans represent the pinnacle of this development. Since whales can do a number of remarkable things that are impossible for terrestrial mammals such as ourselves, let's now take a moment to examine some of these adaptations.

A rare close-up view catches a fin whale in the process of swallowing a meal. The ventral pleats are contracting as the animal strains water through its baleen, trapping the prey on the fringe of hair inside. Despite the enormous size of their mouths, all baleen whales have gullets that are only a few inches across.

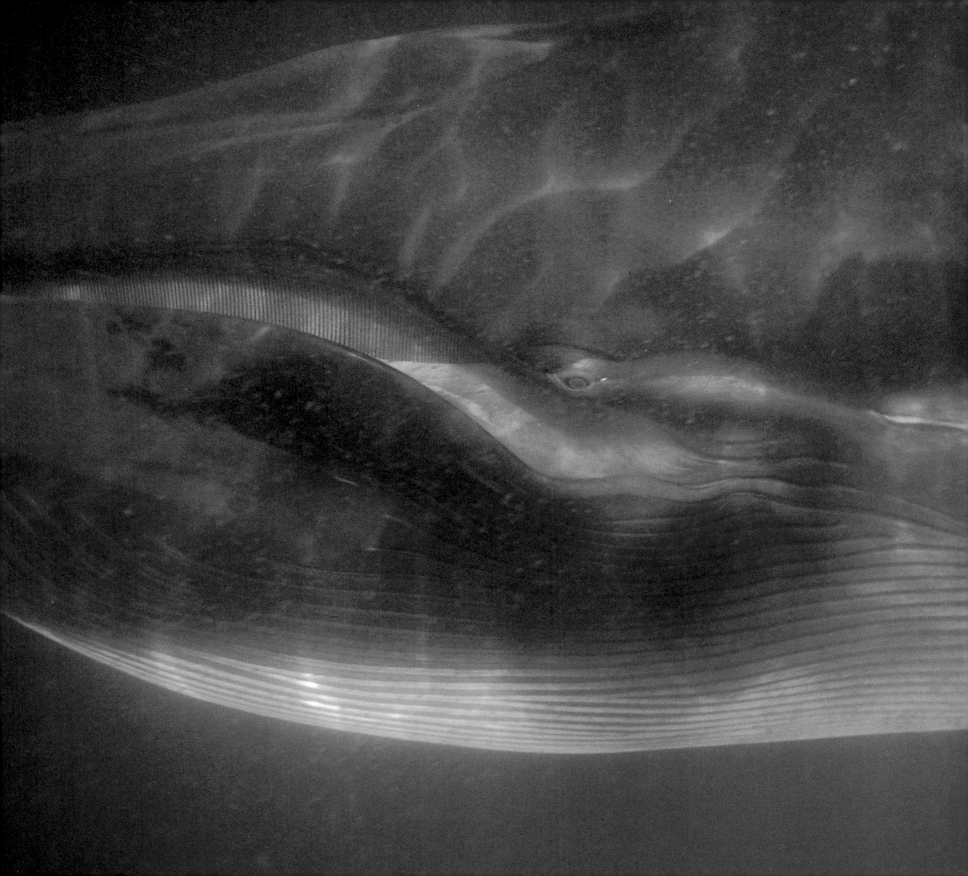

Form and Function

If we compare land animals in respect to magnitude, with those that take up their abode in the deep, we shall find that they will appear contemptible in the comparison. The whale is doubtless the largest animal in creation.

Goldsmith's *Natural History*

Life in the Water: Size and Submergence

Although most cetaceans are not giants, the huge size of the great whales is certainly their most obvious and impressive characteristic. The vast mass attained by both extinct and modern whales can be attributed to life in the water, where gravity has minimal influence. As a result, aquatic animals are free to evolve huge bodies whose weights simply could not be supported on land. The bones of modern whales are lightweight and porous, since heavier skeletal support is not required in the buoyant environment of the oceans. Unfortunately, when cetaceans strand on the coast, this works against them. Subjected to gravity for the first time in its life, a beached whale can crush itself under its own weight.

In all of the baleen whales, females are somewhat larger than males. The opposite is true for many toothed whales, including both orcas and sperm whales. Why female baleen whales should be the larger of the two sexes is not clear, especially since a bias in favor of male size is more usual among mammals. The most commonly offered explanation relates to thermodynamics and the energetics of reproduction: larger female size may be advantageous to conserve heat in cold water while the animal is undergoing the extreme weight loss of lactation, when she will lose about a third of her body weight. Since female sperm whales rarely leave warm water, there is presumably less of a need for larger body size in this species. However, this theory remains unproven.

Although the great bulk of a whale can doom it on land, in the water these animals are unmatched. They ply their way endlessly across the oceans, largely untroubled by even the fiercest of storms. In an instant, they can descend into the unlit depths and remain submerged for periods that are inconceivable to even the most accomplished human divers. This extraordinary diving ability sets whales apart from almost any other mammal. The only rivals are two large seals, the Weddell and elephant seal, which can routinely dive for an hour at a time. However, this feat pales in comparison to the sperm whale, which has been recorded diving for more than two hours, and which can descend to depths of perhaps 10,000 ft (3050 m). The baleen whales are not nearly as accomplished as this. Most can remain underwater for at least 30 minutes, and the bowhead may occasionally dive for an hour, but short dives of a few minutes are much more common in all species.

How can a mammal hold its breath for so long, and at such depth? Interestingly, if we examine the size of a whale's lungs relative to the size of its body, we find that its lungs are proportionately somewhat smaller than our own, but far more efficient. Human lungs exchange about 15–20% of their contents with each breath, whale lungs about 90%. Thus they can take up oxygen and dispose of carbon dioxide much faster than a land animal can.

But there is much more to a whale's diving abilities than this. Although the red blood cells of cetaceans hold about as much oxygen per cell as do ours, a whale has proportionately about one and a half times the blood for its size that we do. Thus it can retain more oxygen, and probably transport it more efficiently, than we land mammals can. Furthermore, about half of this oxygen – much more than in

Huge mouths agape, a group of humpback whales lunges into a school of prey.

humans – is stored in the muscle tissue, using myoglobin (muscle hemoglobin). Myoglobin has a similar capacity for oxygen as regular hemoglobin, but bonds it more tightly. This makes it more difficult for the oxygen to escape back into the bloodstream.

Let us follow a whale as it dives and watch the way in which its physiology works. At the surface, the whale breathes in and out, rapidly taking up air which is distributed in various proportions around the body. As the animal begins its descent, the heart rate slows down, and the blood supply to all but the most vital organs is diminished, allowing the whale to devote the maximum quantity of oxygen to those parts of the body that are most active during a dive. The lungs collapse, minimizing the pressure differential between the inside of the whale's body and the increasing weight of water outside. As the time passes and the oxygen supply within the muscles is used up, the muscles switch to anaerobic respiration, which produces energy without the use of oxygen. Human muscles can also do this, but for rather short periods – a couple of minutes at most. This is because a biproduct of the energy conversion process in anaerobic respiration is something called lactic acid, which causes cramp – our muscles' way of telling us that they lack oxygen, and need circulation restored. In ways that we do not understand, whale muscle can somehow tolerate high levels of lactic acid, and can thus respire without oxygen for protracted periods, allowing the animal to remain underwater for sometimes extraordinary lengths of time. Overall, a whale's physiology is designed to conserve and make maximum use of the oxygen that it takes down with it on a dive.

A dive to even a modest depth involves other problems that must be dealt with. One of these is a remarkable consequence of a whale's size. If even the tallest human beings submerge themselves vertically in the sea, there is little difference in the pressure of the water between their head and their feet. Not so with a whale. Because water pressure increases by one atmosphere for every 30 ft (10 m) of depth, a 100 ft (30 m) blue whale diving straight down will have a difference of three atmospheres between the tip of its head and the trailing edge of its huge tail. What's more, this pressure will constantly change as the animal descends to greater depths. To appreciate what a problem this is for the whale's body fluids, imagine a large balloon filled with water. If you create a pressure differential by squeezing the bottom part of the balloon, the water inevitably moves upwards. While this doesn't matter to a balloon, it can be a major problem for the blood of a whale, since forced movement of such vital fluids away from places where they are needed can be dangerous or even fatal.

How do whales deal with this unique difficulty? The answer lies in a remarkable system of valves within a whale's circulatory system. Known as the *retia mirabile* ('wonderful nets'), these complex valve systems are unique in mammals, and work to regulate the flow of blood even under the intense and rapidly changing pressures of a dive. The circulation itself is of course driven by the vast heart, which beats very slowly: in a large whale, the heart rate is probably about seven or eight beats a minute, and less during a dive.

Pressure also brings other dangers. If a human scuba diver returns to the surface too rapidly from even 100 ft (30 m), he runs the risk of a dangerous condition known as 'the bends'. Nitrogen, an inert gas that makes up the majority of the air we breathe, is put under pressure by the weight of water at depth. A rapid ascent has the effect of depressurizing the nitrogen in the blood, causing it to form bubbles, and the result is the bends. A good analogy is what happens when you pressurize the contents of a can of soda by shaking it, then remove the top. The gas in the soda (in this case carbon dioxide) reacts to the sudden decrease in pressure by forming bubbles. When this happens to nitrogen in the blood, it can be fatal.

How do whales avoid the bends? We are not entirely sure, but we know part of the answer. A diving whale takes with it only a few lungfuls of air, and therefore the quantity of nitrogen in its blood is quite limited. By contrast, a human diver obtains a constantly fresh supply of air, and therefore of nitrogen, from his scuba tank. Worse, the air in the tank is already under pressure, which exacerbates the problem in the blood. The relatively small quantity of unpressurized nitrogen in a

A sperm whale hangs motionless just below the surface. We know virtually nothing of the intelligence of this fascinating and most ancient of cetaceans. However, its social organization is highly complex, and the sperm whale's huge skull encloses the largest brain of any animal on Earth.

The head and open mouth of a young gray whale, showing the tongue and part of the baleen that hangs down from the upper jaw. Baleen evolved millions of years ago in ancient toothed whales, and provides modern mysticetes with the means to exploit the most abundant food in the ocean, zooplankton and small schooling fish.

Baleen varies considerably in size and form among different species of whales. In some, such as this gray whale, it is relatively short, while in others (like the right whale and the bowhead) it can be very long. The inner fringe of hair that serves as the filtration mechanism also varies from fine to coarse, depending on whether the whale's diet consists of smaller or larger organisms.

In the gray whale, exceptionally thick, strong baleen is needed to prevent breakage during bottom-feeding, when the animal's mouth is in frequent contact with the sea floor. Since gray whales generally show a preference for rolling on a particular side when they feed along the bottom, the baleen is usually much more worn and warped on that side than on the other.

diving whale's body is probably the main reason that whales do not suffer from diving sickness, although the full explanation is undoubtedly more complicated than this.

All whales are great divers by our standards, but baleen whales generally do not dive to more than a few hundred feet. Beaked whales and sperm whales, however, routinely descend into truly abyssal depths.

Food and Feeding

Now that we have examined the mechanism by which whales dive, let's consider how they actually operate in this strange place so remote from the sunlit world that we know. Hunting is a major activity for these animals. Some, like most of the baleen whales, feed for only part of the year. Others eat year-round and do not undergo seasonal fasts. Baleen whales, despite their huge size, feed on small schooling fish or tiny planktonic organisms. Sperm whales take larger fish and squid (sometimes very large squid), while some killer whales eat other marine mammals.

The first step in feeding is obviously to find your food. For sperm whales and other odontocetes, this involves the use of a highly sophisticated biological sonar: the animal sends out high-frequency pulses of sound, and by analyzing the returning echoes can locate prey that is well beyond its range of vision. It is quite likely that a toothed whale's sonar is so advanced that, like ultrasound, the animal has the ability to 'see' in sound, scanning even the internal structure of living things. This remarkable echolocation system permits sperm whales to obtain a clear picture of their surroundings, even in the utterly lightless world of the great depths. Although evidence suggests that vision is quite good in most cetaceans, it is certainly not the primary sense in odontocetes.

Our understanding of prey detection in baleen whales is not nearly as good. As far as we can tell, baleen whales do not possess sonar, at least not the high-frequency echolocation that is characteristic of the odontocetes. It is very probable that whales do not search randomly. Rather they will know, from experience and oceanographic cues, areas in which food is most likely to occur. Once there, however, it is not at all clear how they actually locate schools of fish or plankton. One interesting difference between toothed and baleen whales is that the latter probably still possess a fairly well-developed sense of smell. The olfactory lobe of the brain is quite large in the mysticetes, whereas in the toothed whales it is rudimentary. This makes sense, since an animal that has such an efficient sonar system would hardly need a sense of smell, especially since odors are largely undetectable underwater. For baleen whales, however, smell may play an important role in finding food, when that food is present in concentrations at the surface. Anyone who has stood downwind of a large patch of plankton will tell you that it gives off a noticeable odor, and there is no reason to suppose that whales would not take advantage of this cue to locate either the plankton itself or small fish that are feeding on it. Most of the time, however, a whale's food is beneath the surface, and we simply do not know how they find it.

Once prey has been located, its mode of ingestion varies between baleen and toothed whales. The latter almost certainly use suction when taking in food. Since no odontocete has molars, there is no chewing of food – it is swallowed whole.

Baleen whales have no teeth at all, and instead filter their food in various ways. Each whale has, depending on the species, a variable number of hard baleen plates hanging down from the upper jaws in two huge racks, one on either side of the mouth. The inner surface of the plates is fringed with hair. A feeding whale first takes into its mouth a huge volume of water and food. In rorquals, the pleats on the underside of the body expand like an accordion at this time, allowing the whale to greatly increase the capacity of its mouth. Using its tongue and sometimes other means, the whale then forces the water out of the mouth. Although the water can easily pass through the narrow spaces between each of the hundreds of baleen plates, the prey is trapped on the inner fringe of hair. This accomplished, the whale simply swallows. One of the interesting features of all mysticetes is that, while the mouth can be truly vast, the throat is very small. In even large blue whales, it is just a few inches wide, a reflection of the fact that these great animals feed upon small organisms.

The baleen fringe varies considerably from species to species. In right whales, it is silky and fine, since it must trap tiny creatures like copepods. In humpback whales, which feed on fish and krill, the fringe is quite coarse, since a fine-mesh strainer is not required for these larger prey items.

There are three basic feeding modes among the baleen whales. 'Gulpers' take in one large mouthful of water and food, strain the water, swallow the food, then move on to another 'gulp'. Gulpers include all the rorquals. By contrast, 'skimmers' do not feed in discrete events, but rather move with mouth open through a patch of prey, continuously filtering as they swim. Right and bowhead whales feed in this manner, as does the versatile sei whale – the only rorqual that is both a gulper and skimmer. Bottom-feeding is the third method. This is practiced primarily by gray whales, who move along the ocean floor and suction large quantities of benthic creatures from the sediment.

Digestion and Metabolism

If they could survive the trip, any hapless prey swallowed by a whale would find themselves entering a four-chambered digestive system that more closely resembles that of a herbivore than a carnivore. In cows and other ruminants, the forestomach undertakes the initial breakdown of the food, and this is accomplished with the help of a vast population of bacteria. Scientists generally doubted that such a symbiotic relationship existed in large whales simply because no such bacteria could be found. However, there is now good evidence from at least gray whales that such intestinal fauna exist, so bacterial degradation of food may indeed occur in some species.

Pound for pound, cetaceans consume more energy than typical terrestrial mammals, probably because they are constantly on the move. A large baleen whale will eat perhaps 3 or 4% of its own weight each day during the feeding season, which can translate into several tons of fish, krill or plankton.

A major specialization evolved by early cetaceans was the ability to extract fresh water from prey, and to deal with the problems posed by intake of salt. Since cetaceans have no sweat glands, and since they exist in a very saline medium, their kidneys must function far more efficiently than do ours. The kidneys of most cetaceans are proportionately twice the size of a terrestrial mammal's, and far more specialized. It is likely that, as a result of the need to eliminate large quantities of salt from their bodies, cetaceans produce more urine than land animals.

Fat and Heat

From its food, a whale obtains fat, which is stored in the blubber, among other places. Since whales often exist quite comfortably in near-freezing water temperatures that would kill us in a few moments, it is obvious that their insulation is highly efficient; in fact they sometimes need to shed heat. In migratory species which travel to tropical waters in winter (the humpback, for example), this problem can be quite acute, notably when an animal is highly active. Excess heat is lost in various ways, the most common of which involves the whale increasing blood flow to extremities such as the flippers, tail and dorsal fin, all of which act rather like a radiator. Passing close to the surface of the skin, the blood sheds some of its heat energy into the cooler water of the ocean.

Reproduction

All sexual reproduction begins with mating. This is not uncommonly observed in right whales and gray whales, both of which sometimes copulate at the surface; but there are few or no reliable observations of this most fundamental of acts in other species. Most mating probably happens underwater, and is believed to be rapid.

Since whales must minimize drag in the water, all genitalia are internal. In males, both the penis and testes lie within the body, although the former organ is retractable and is extruded during mating. The

A blue whale caught in the act of feeding. The normally streamlined underside has ballooned out as the ventral pleats expand, allowing the whale to greatly increase the capacity of its mouth. During this process, the whale's huge tongue drops through a cavity in the floor of the animal's mouth, and works to assist with the expansion and subsequent contraction of the pleats.

penis is actually fibroelastic, not vascular as it is in primates like humans, and it has a surprisingly mobile tip. Since at least right and gray whales can mate side by side, the penis must be capable of extending over the body of the female to initiate copulation.

Pregnancy in sperm whales lasts about 17 months. In most baleen whales, by contrast, it is a little less than a year. Producing a huge calf in so short a time is no mean feat, and the fetal growth rate of mysticetes is the fastest in the animal kingdom, some twenty times that of primates. A blue or fin whale calf will double its mass in the last two months of gestation, a growth rate that is quite astonishing in light of the demands it must make on the calf's development, not to mention on the mother! This telescoping of gestation into less than a year was most likely an evolutionary response to migratory needs.

Birth, which has been observed even more rarely than mating, is very probably quick. Single births are most common. Although the frequency of multiple fetuses varies a little among species, these (mainly twins) were on average observed in fewer than 2% of pregnant females examined from whaling catches. Because lactation imposes huge energetic demands upon the mother, the chances of a female successfully raising two or more offspring at a time seem small. There is no reliable record of a whale seen at sea with twin calves.

Lactation is so expensive because of the high fat content of the milk. In humpback whales, it is around 35%, almost ten times that of human milk or cow's milk. The milk is delivered through two mammary glands, one on either side of the female's genital slit. Unlike terrestrial mammals, whales have a compressor muscle in each mammary gland, which is used to pump milk into the mouth of the nursing calf. Whales babies drink huge quantities of milk: in the case of a blue whale, the mother may deliver more than a 100 gallons (380 liters) a day.

Brain and Intelligence: Are Whales Really Smart?

To some people, whales are seen as highly evolved beings. To others, they are more akin to swimming cows. Which is correct?

To some extent the answer depends upon how one defines and measures intelligence. Since we cannot test the IQ of a large whale, we must look at the size and structure of the brain. Absolute size is of little value, since large-bodied animals will often have large brains. Relative size is more informative, and here we find considerable differences among cetaceans. Generally, toothed whales have proportionately larger brains relative to their body size than baleen whales. In some dolphins, the relative brain size approaches that of humans.

Another possible measure is the development of the brain, and here again toothed whales generally appear to be more advanced than mysticetes, having a greater number of convolutions and a more developed frontal cortex. However, it has been argued that, since dolphins and sperm whales possess such an advanced sonar system, much of their brains is given over to the processing of acoustic information. Overall, too little is known about brain function in cetaceans to draw any definitive conclusions.

My own opinion, formed from years of observing cetaceans, is similar to that of many scientists. As a general rule, toothed whales seem smarter than baleen whales (which in many ways really do seem like aquatic cows in their lifestyle and problem-solving abilities). It is tempting to look at the complex social system of sperm whales and killer whales and deduce that this is evidence of high intelligence. It may well be; but I for one would not care to speculate on the nature and degree of that intelligence, nor on how these animals see the world. I rather doubt that any whales are gifted with extraordinary intelligence. But, when all is said and done, cetaceans exist in an environment that is completely foreign to us, and it is probably vain to judge their intelligence by standards peculiar to our human world.

The sleek back of a large fin whale breaks the surface as the animal comes up to breathe. The whale's vertebrae are clearly visible along the midline.

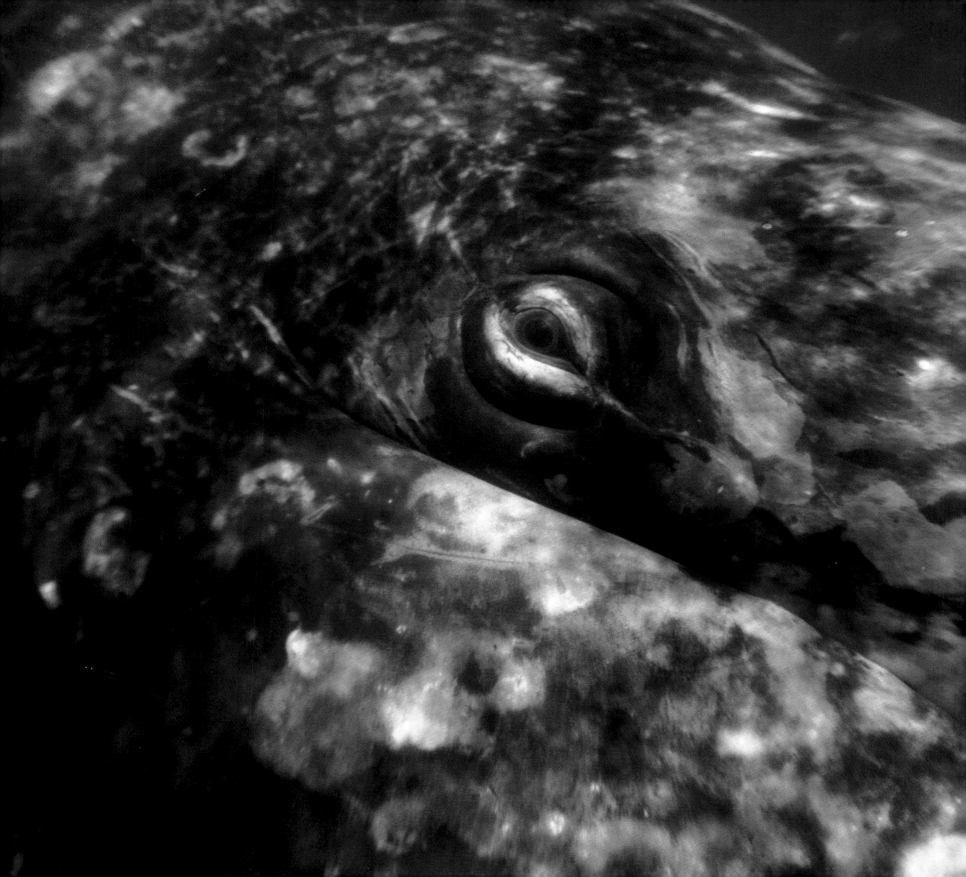

The Great Wanderers

Oh, the rare old Whale,
mid storm and gale
In his ocean will be
A giant in might,
where might is right
And King of the boundless sea.
Anonymous

With the changing of the seasons from autumn to winter, or from winter to spring, baleen whales all over the world begin to execute a grand movement that will take them thousands of miles to different waters. Not all species are highly migratory: the bowhead makes limited migrations associated with changes in sea ice, and some Bryde's whales do not migrate at all. But most of the baleen whales will, during the course of their long lives, travel many times between the cold waters of high latitudes and the warmth of the tropics. In sperm whales, males undertake long journeys from polar waters to low latitudes, where they seek out females for breeding; the females themselves rarely leave warm water.

Some of these extraordinary migrations are the longest undertaken by any mammal. Both humpbacks and gray whales are known to travel as much as 5000 miles (8000 km) in one direction, a journey which takes them through many environmental changes. But why do they do this? Remarkably, we cannot yet answer this fundamental question.

Migration is a common feature of the life cycles of many animals and birds. In most cases, it is undertaken to secure better feeding grounds during the winter months. However, this is not the case with migratory baleen whales, most of which appear to fast while in tropical waters. This is not by choice: instead, tropical waters are in most cases highly unproductive relative to those of high latitudes. To understand why, we have to look at some of the basic biological and oceanographic processes that occur in marine systems.

Productivity in Marine Systems

The waters of many cold-water regions seasonally undergo what is known as 'turnover'. During summer, the water becomes stratified as the sun heats the upper layer which 'sits' upon colder, denser layers that the sun's energy does not reach. In winter, the exposed upper layer cools more rapidly than the one below it, eventually becoming colder and denser, which causes it to sink. This mixing is aided by storms, and by hydrographic features such as underwater banks which facilitate an important process known as 'upwelling'. The mixing is critical, because it returns to the surface nutrients that have fallen to the sea floor. These nutrients are utilized by phytoplankton, the microscopic plants that form the foundation of all marine food chains. The phytoplankton reproduce in vast numbers, supporting populations of zooplankton (literally, 'animal plankton'). These tiny animals in turn become food for other creatures, including some whales or the small fish that are themselves cetacean prey. Without the turnover and the upwelling of nutrients, the phytoplankton become nutrient-limited, and the biomass which they can support remains relatively small.

In tropical waters, where there is far less variation in temperature during the year, the upper layers of water never become cold enough to sink. Thus the water column is permanently stratified, and nutrients do not return to the surface in abundance. The relatively unproductive nature of much tropical water is reflected in its clarity, which is due to the low density of plankton. Although we can find many species of fish in the tropics, the system generally cannot support the huge biomass of prey that exists in high latitudes (sperm whales get around this restriction by feeding on abundant deep-water squid).

Why Migrate?

So migratory baleen whales must fast during winter, subsisting instead on the large fat reserves that they have built up during the summer feeding season in high latitudes. Why, then, do they migrate at all?

There are various theories, none of them proven. An old idea – that migration represents a return to ancestral breeding grounds – seems implausible, since evolution tends to select against costly behaviors that serve no real purpose. The most popular theory suggests that migration is a balancing act between the need to exploit seasonal pulses of productivity in high latitudes during summer, and the thermodynamic advantages of spending the winter in warm water. As intuitively reasonable as this idea sounds, it has many critics. Why would such a massive, well-insulated animal as a whale need to leave cold water when that same frigid environment is often host to much smaller warm-blooded creatures? In one variation of the theory, the main advantage to wintering in warm water accrues to newborn calves, who are not protected from the cold by as much blubber as older animals. But if this is true, why does the rest of the population have to follow suit? One version of the basic idea maintains that large body size is itself a vital component of this behavior, since it allows the whale to store vast reserves of fat that will sustain it through the winter while conserving energy in warm water.

Our acceptance of this theory of migration hinges upon the answer to a single question. In a cost-benefit energetic analysis, do whales benefit overall by conserving heat in warm water even though they are not eating, or would they do better to remain in cold water and perhaps be able to feed at least some of the time? At this point we do not know, largely because values for several of the key variables involved in such an analysis are not available.

Whatever the ultimate reason for migration, it is becoming clear that not all members of a population necessarily migrate every year. We are a long way from understanding the individual life history strategies that dictate whether a whale will leave the feeding grounds during winter. Nonetheless, given the varying demands and opportunities imposed by differences in an animal's sex, age and reproductive condition, we should not be surprised to find individual variation within the migratory habits of a species.

Contrasts and Connections: the Strong Influence of Migration

Although we cannot know for certain why baleen whales migrate, we do know that these great seasonal movements radically affect many aspects of the animals' biology and behavior. In migratory baleen whales, gestation has been telescoped into about a year – a remarkably short period given the size of the offspring. As we have seen, the fetal growth rate is astonishingly rapid as a result. We know that lactation is very expensive in baleen whales; in light of this, many scientists believe that the short gestation period is driven by the necessity to time birth so that it permits the mother to take maximum advantage of seasonal pulses in productivity on the feeding grounds.

Strongly seasonal breeding is the rule in all mysticetes except a coastal form of the Bryde's whale. The latter is unusual both in its year-round residency in tropical waters, and in the apparent lack of seasonality in its reproduction. That these animals have succeeded in colonizing an ecological niche that permits feeding throughout the year, and that they also breed year-round, is a strong argument for the link between seasonal feeding, seasonal reproduction and migratory timing in other species.

For many migratory whales, the year is sharply divided both geographically and behaviorally. Humpback whales exemplify these seasonal contrasts. In summer, they feed in high latitudes, but do not mate. In winter, they travel to tropical waters where they mate and calve, but do not eat for periods of weeks or even months. Furthermore, frequent cooperation between foraging animals on the

*In the cold air of an Alaskan morning, the blows of two humpback whales hang above the
animals as they begin another dive sequence. Like most baleen whales, humpbacks spend the summer
in the cold waters of high latitudes, sometimes traveling well above the Arctic or Antarctic circle in their
search for food. Once they have left the feeding grounds in late autumn, the whales cease eating
and will fast for up to several months during their winter sojourn in the tropics.*

*A gray whale mother and calf travel closely together as they begin
the 5000-mile (8000-km) migration that will take them from Baja California to the rich
feeding grounds of the Bering Sea. At 13 months, the gray whale's gestation
period is among the longest of any baleen whale.*

feeding grounds breaks down in winter as male humpbacks compete aggressively for access to females.

When to Leave, and How to Get There

What tells a whale that it is time to migrate, and how do they successfully navigate across vast stretches of open ocean to return to the same feeding and breeding areas year after year? It is not clear whether migration is initiated in response to seasonal environmental changes, or to some internal cue. The diminishing daylight of autumn is one obvious possibility, although since this will change significantly with latitude it cannot be a simple relationship. Changes in water temperature will be similarly relative: a humpback whale in the Gulf of Maine in August may feed in water as warm as 70° Fahrenheit (21° Celsius), while another summering off Greenland will rarely experience a temperature higher than a couple of degrees above freezing.

It is possible that a complex feedback loop exists within a whale's body that somehow links fat levels or other indicators to migratory timing. For example, perhaps changing hormonal levels cue newly pregnant females to leave the breeding grounds. However, we can do little more than speculate about the physiological details of such a mechanism. A combination of both external and internal cues in prompting migratory behavior is not unlikely, but our understanding of such interactions is currently poor.

Whatever causes a whale to begin the migration, the animal is faced with finding its way over a great distance, generally over open water with few obvious points of reference. At least, few that are obvious to us.

There are at least three means of navigation that may be available to whales. The first involves the ability to detect the Earth's magnetic field and use it as a map or a compass. The magnetic field strength varies from place to place, containing highs and lows like hills and valleys in the visible landscape. Fault lines and their associated magnetic fields may act as magnetic 'highways' for animals to follow, and there is good evidence that migrating birds use such features to find their way.

Detection of the field requires a 'magnetoreceptor' called biomagnetite, a chemical found in the brains of many migratory species, including some whales. While proof of biomagnetic navigation is hard to obtain, the existence of such a capability in some cetaceans seems quite plausible.

Indeed, Dr Margaret Klinowska has suggested that many mass strandings (notably of pilot whales, *Globicephala melaena*) are due to navigational errors made by the whales in regions characterized by anomalies in the Earth's magnetic field. This idea is intriguing, but it remains unproven and the subject of much debate.

It has also been proposed that whales which migrate close to coastlines may find their way by periodically searching for familiar landmarks. This has been suggested for gray whales migrating along the western coast of North America, who are occasionally observed to spyhop (raise their heads out of the water) as if scanning the coastline. We do not know whether this idea is correct, and it raises the question of how good a whale's eyesight is. After all, the lens in a whale's eye is designed to accommodate the refractive index of water. Because this index is different from that of air, it is possible that whales become near-sighted when gazing around above the surface.

The third navigational possibility is one that would have been deemed fiction even a few years ago. Blue and fin whales make very loud sounds at very low frequencies, and these sounds can easily travel hundreds of miles or more in deep water. As we will see later on, it has recently been suggested that one of the functions of these booming vocalizations is to echolocate over great distances. It is not implausible that these extraordinary animals locate specific islands or seamounts from hundreds of miles away by bouncing sounds off them and listening for the returning echoes.

We do not know how whales unerringly find their way back to the same places in the vast ocean every year. Probably they use a combination of navigational methods, woven together with knowledge of currents, hydrography and other features, knowledge that is supplemented with every migration, and with each year of the animal's life.

Whale Societies

Any keen observer who has spent a day with whales will learn a good deal about their social behavior. If our observer is spending her day with baleen whales, she will most likely note that many individuals appear to be alone in their activities, or that they associate with others for relatively short periods. If sperm whales or killer whales are her subjects, she will be struck by the remarkable cohesion of their groups.

Although the social system of whales varies from species to species, some generalizations can be made. Overall, odontocetes are more obviously social than baleen whales. Many species of toothed whales travel in groups that remain together for long periods. In the case of some killer whales and perhaps pilot whales, these bonds may endure for the lives of all group members. In these animals and in sperm whales, long-term bonds, prolonged maternal care, and perhaps even sharing of accumulated knowledge seem to be the primary social strategies. Kinship (associations between relatives) is of fundamental importance in the social life of many species.

By contrast, baleen whales rarely form stable associations. If our observer were to follow a baleen whale for a day or two, she would generally find that it spent much of its time alone, or changed associates quite frequently. For many years, scientists often described baleen whale social organization as random. We now know that this is not the case, but it required many years of careful observations to show that, while mysticete social structure is not tight-knit, it does contain recognizable patterns. However, there is minimal maternal investment in offspring, and kinship probably plays only a minor role in social interactions.

What is a Group?

The correct collective noun for a group of whales or dolphins is a pod. But what exactly makes up a pod? This is not a trivial question, and we must be careful in our definitions. A commonly applied definition is that a pod is any group of two or more animals who travel side by side, and who generally coordinate their speed and direction of movement.

This most obvious level of association is used by scientists when recording social behavior. For example, a group of sperm whales will remain together as a unit. They will sometimes stagger their diving schedules so that only some members of the group are at the surface at a time, but overall they coordinate their activities and their travels with remarkable cohesion. They may associate with other pods for periods of time, forming a larger group, but eventually this assemblage will segregate into its component units, which will go their separate ways. Similarly, when we see several baleen whales traveling together we call them a pod, and when its members separate, as often happens, we no longer consider them associated.

If we were dealing with many terrestrial mammals, we could be quite confident of our definitions. On land, it is often easy to observe aggregations of animals moving loosely together, and to recognize that they constitute a herd, or to rule out such large-scale associations within an aggregation. Not so with whales. In general, when many baleen whales are found together in the same place they are considered to be drawn there solely by their interest in a common resource, notably food. We can recognize small groups within the aggregation, but the overall coordination that on land would define the assemblage as a herd appears to be absent.

Protective of her calf, a humpback whale mother keeps a wary eye on the photographer as the pair passes by.

Although this working definition is very useful, we do not know if it is correct. A major difference between cetaceans and most terrestrial animals is a whale's ability to communicate over considerable distances. Sound travels five times faster in water than in air, and acoustic signals are much less likely to fade out in an aquatic medium. Under the right conditions, certain vocalizations can travel hundreds of miles or more. Blue and fin whales make very loud, very low-frequency sounds that have been heard at distances exceeding 1500 miles (2400 km). Although such extreme transmission is possible only in deep water, and only at low frequencies, certain other whale sounds can travel for several miles in even quite shallow water.

This, then, is the problem. We are dealing with animals that may be able to remain in acoustic contact over distances that exceed the visual range of our observations. In the deep ocean environment, some large whales may hear each other over hundreds of miles. In the face of this, our common-sense definition of a group begins to look very dubious. Do whales that are separated by miles ever move as a group? We do not know, but this represents a fascinating area for future research.

The Ties That Bind: Ecology and Social Behavior

Another approach to understanding the social structure of cetaceans is to examine their ecology. In essence, we can take what we know about their food, predation and environment and try to predict what social system should exist given these characteristics. We know that social systems do not develop randomly, but rather in response to ecology. For example, groups often form to increase feeding efficiency or to better detect or defend against predators. Unpredictably distributed, patchy food resources often result in groups that change size frequently. Ultimately, the size and stability of a group will represent a trade-off between the various costs and benefits of remaining together or staying apart.

In many species, stable groups consist primarily of related animals. This is because close relatives share at least some genes; therefore,

since reproductive success is measured by how many copies of one's genes are passed to future generations, one can indirectly increase one's own success by helping a relative improve theirs. But even here there are costs: if group size exceeds the number that can be supported by available resources, members will not benefit and splits may occur. This situation is observed in killer whales, in which maternally related pods grow with the birth of new calves. Eventually, fission occurs as specific mature females and their offspring leave to form their own groups.

Killer whales also represent a prime example of cooperation in foraging. Those orcas that feed on marine mammals will often hunt together. There is evidence for some division of labor in these hunts. My colleague Howard Rosenbaum describes an attack by orcas on a group of three humpback whales that included a mother, calf and escort. The mature male killer whales harassed the adults while the females and juveniles managed to isolate the calf. It is not clear whether the calf was killed in this instance, since rough weather made following the group very difficult; but the calf was not observed again. Killer whales may also teach hunting techniques to their young, although the existence of true 'teaching' (i.e. the intentional transmission of knowledge from parent to offspring) among animals is controversial.

A different form of foraging cooperation exists among many baleen whales. Here, prey is always found in patches of variable size, whether it is a school of small fish, a shoal of krill or a patch of tiny zooplankton such as copepods. Often, these patches are too small to support more than one whale, and animals are observed feeding alone. When prey schools are large, however, many whales may feed together. In the case of humpback whales, several animals will sometimes work in concert to blow the well-known bubble clouds or bubble nets that trap schooling fish.

Predation has a huge impact on the social ecology of most species of animals. It has been the evolutionary force behind the development of innumerable adaptations, ranging from group defence to camou-

A group of killer whales travels through northern waters off British Columbia, Canada. The two mature males (center and extreme right) are easily identifiable by their huge dorsal fins, which are each about 6 ft (2 m) tall. Killer whales appear to remain with their families for their entire lives.

flage. It is not clear how much large whales have to fear from preda-tors. Attacks by orcas on even blue whales are occasionally observed, and are sometimes fatal. The tails and bodies of many humpback whales show rake-mark scars which are presumed to have come from killer whale teeth. However, it seems that most of these attacks are not serious, or are perhaps testing the vulnerability of the intended prey. My own belief is that large whales do not live under constant threat of predation. If fatal attacks do occur, they most probably involve young calves, perhaps on migration.

Certainly, the social structure of baleen whales does not resemble that of species that must be constantly on the alert for predators. Stable groups (which one might expect for enhanced alertness or defense) are rare. With the exception of gray whales, we know little about group size and behavior during migration, when calves must be particularly vulnerable to attack. The ocean environment is highly opaque, and predators such as killer whales cannot visually detect prey over anything other than very short distances. Thus, it may be advantageous for baleen whales to migrate alone and silently rather than in large groups.

Mating Systems

Mammals have a wide variety of mating systems. Most are polygynous in some form (males mate with many females) or promiscuous (both sexes mate with several partners). In a few species, females will mate with multiple males, sometimes in quick succession. True monogamy, while quite common in birds, is rare among mammals.

It is important to realize that not all species go about the business of reproduction in the same way. Male humpback whales fight over females, and also use songs to attract potential mates (and perhaps to keep other males at a distance). Overt aggression appears rare in male right whales; instead, a female will sometimes allow several males to copulate with her, and much of the competition occurs among their sperm. Right whales have huge testes, almost certainly to pro-duce large amounts of sperm in an attempt to outcompete other

males who have recently inseminated the same female.

Some baleen whales aggregate during the breeding season; these include gray whales, right whales and humpbacks. These concentra-tions can be huge: Silver Bank off the Dominican Republic is the largest humpback whale breeding ground in the world, and probably hosts some 3000 animals at the height of the season. Other species may disperse; in the case of blue and fin whales, this may be related to the long-range calls which they are capable of producing.

With the advent of new genetic techniques, it is likely that we will soon understand a great deal more about the mating systems of whales than we currently do. Dr Per Palsbøll and I have recently used genetic techniques to determine that, when individual female hump-backs have several calves over a number of years, they are fathered by different males (i.e. females do not mate with the same partner in dif-ferent breeding seasons). There is also a suggestion in our data that related male humpbacks cooperate to fight for access to females, an idea that has recently gained support from a genetic study by Dr Elena Valsecchi.

We know relatively little about the mating system of large toothed whales. It is widely assumed that male sperm whales will sometimes fight over mating rights, as evidenced in old wounds that may be as serious as a broken lower jaw. The old idea that sperm whale groups contained a 'harem master' male that mated with all the females now seems incorrect. Recent work has shown that different males visit pods of females, but we do not know whether all the calves in a par-ticular group are sired by one or several fathers. The same questions apply to killer whales, although here long-term observations of identi-fied individuals have given us many insights into the social structure of the species.

Certainly much remains to be learned about social behavior in whales. Our knowledge of this and other topics varies by species, ranging from quite good to extremely poor. But, having covered the basics of whale biology, let's now look at what we know about the life and behavior of each of these remarkable animals.

Sperm whales have one of the more complex social systems of any mammal. Traveling in tightly knit groups that are based at least in part upon kinship, they maintain close acoustic contact even while spread out on foraging dives to great depths. During these forays, animals in the group will vary their dive schedules so that at least one adult is always available to 'babysit' calves at the surface. Each sperm whale has a unique acoustic signature, known as a coda, by which others in the group can recognize it.

Around the age of six years, a male sperm whale will leave his natal group and travel to polar waters. There, he will remain until he has reached adulthood, when he will return to the tropics to seek out females for breeding. Young females, by contrast, appear to remain in warm water for most of their lives.

Blue Whale

There is no whaler or whale biologist, no matter how jaded, whose heart does not race at the sight of a blue whale.

Dr Dale Rice

Scientific name: *Balaenoptera musculus* ('winged whale' + either 'muscular' or 'mouse'. Given the animal's size, the latter meaning may have been a joke on the part of Linnaeus, who named this species). The so-called pygmy blue whale, *Balaenoptera musculus brevicauda* (= 'short tail') is widely recognized as a valid subspecies.

Other common names: sulfur-bottom whale.

Maximum length: 110 ft (33 m). Females up to 10 ft (3 m) larger than males.

Distribution: all oceans.

General Characteristics

A giant among giants, the blue whale is the largest animal ever to have lived in the history of life on Earth. As long as the longest dinosaur and several times its mass, blue whales can attain lengths exceeding 100 ft (30 m) and weights of close to 200 tons. Seeing a blue whale up close is one of the most exciting spectacles in Nature.

There is some disagreement about the largest blue whale on record. There is a record of a 110-ft (33.5-m) female taken off the island of South Georgia in 1909, but not everyone accepts that this animal was accurately measured. The report of a 103-ft (31.3-m) female from the same period is not disputed; but at these sizes a difference of a few feet is frankly irrelevant. Given that the blue whale has been on Earth for several million years, it is quite likely that the population has boasted 110-ft (33.5-m) animals at some point in the past.

All our concepts of scale have to be revised when we are dealing with blue whales; everything about them is unimaginably vast.

At 100 ft (30 m), a blue whale would weigh close to 200 tons. One 100-ft female that was cut up and weighed in pieces came in at 179 tons, exclusive of blood lost during the butchering process – and it is not unlikely that an animal of this size would contain 10 or 20 tons of blood. The size of the animal's internal organs is mind-boggling. Consider that the heart of a blue whale is an organ exactly the same as our own in its basic structure and function; in fact, the heart is no larger than ours when measured as a proportion of the body size. In absolute terms, however, it is huge: approximately the size of an automobile. A blue whale's arteries are so large that a baby could crawl through them with room to spare.

Blue whales are undeniably beautiful animals. Appearing as a mottled gray at the surface, they take on a quite lovely blue color when seen underwater. Their bodies are often covered with a film of diatoms, giving their pale bellies a yellowish tinge; hence they were commonly known to the whalers as 'sulfur-bottoms'. The head is broad and U-shaped, and the huge nostrils are set behind a high splashguard. From this great nose comes the greatest blow of any whale. I once saw, in the still clear air of a gray Greenland day, a group of blue whales blowing about 9 miles (14 km) away; I would not be surprised if some of the larger spouts were 50 or 60 ft (15 or 20 m) tall.

The long, sleek body seems to roll forever when the whale is beginning to dive. After what can seem like an unending quantity of back passing by, the tiny dorsal fin comes into view, followed by the long peduncle and sometimes the great tail. Unlike their close relative the finback, blue whales often raise their tails during a dive.

The vast mouth contains between 520 and 900 plates of baleen, and these plates are uniformly black in color. The mouth also houses a huge tongue which can weigh many tons. There are from 55 to 68 pleats on the underside of the body, running, as in all rorquals, from just below the chin almost to the whale's umbilicus.

Distribution and Movements

Blue whales are found in all the oceans of the world. Like most rorquals, they migrate annually between high-latitude feeding grounds and mating and calving areas in warm waters. However, the population structure is not entirely clear: in some tropical areas, blue whales are observed in all months, suggesting either a year-round residence by one population or overlapping seasonal occupancy by two. An example of this occurs in the Pacific off Costa Rica, and it has been suggested that some of the blue whales seen there originate in the southern hemi-sphere.

Our knowledge of the distribution and movements of this whale is complicated by the existence of a subspecies, the pygmy blue – hardly an appropriate name for an animal that attains a length of more than 85 ft (26 m). Pygmy blue whales are morphologically different from 'true' blue whales, most noticeably in that the caudal peduncle (tail stock) is shorter. Pygmy blue whales were thought to be confined to the Indian Ocean region, but recent examination of blue whales from elsewhere suggests that their distribution may be more widespread.

Life History

Like most baleen whales, the breeding season of the blue whale is strongly seasonal, with a gestation period of about 11 months. At the end of this time, in late winter, a blue whale mother gives birth to the largest baby on Earth. Blue whale calves are on average 26 ft (8 m) long at birth, with a weight of perhaps 4 tons. Nursed by a daily diet of per-haps 100 gallons (350 liters) of fat-rich milk, they grow at an astonishing rate of an inch or more (2 or 3 cm) a day before being weaned at about seven months.

The development of a blue whale calf from a barely visible ovum at conception to a 50-ft (15-m) juvenile at weaning represents the fastest growth rate in the animal kingdom: it is an increase in tissue of several billion-fold in a little more than a year and a half.

Both males and females are sexually mature at approximately five to six years, and females produce a single calf every two or three years. We do not know how long blue whales live, although given the great longevity of their close relative the finback, it seems likely that they can also reach ages of 70 years or more. This century, however, few blue whales have been afforded the opportunity to live out their lives to their natural end.

Diet

Blue whales eat more than any other creature on Earth. Feeding almost exclusively on krill, they probably ingest 3 or 4% of their own weight each day during the feeding season. For the largest females, this may mean a daily consumption of 6 to 8 tons of food. The krill is captured by pure speed: blue whales are fast animals, and will simply accelerate into a school of krill and engulf it before most of the prey has a chance to escape. Blue whales have occasionally been observed feeding on shoals of pelagic red crabs, but this is rare; it is clear that this mysticete is almost entirely dependent upon euphausiids.

Social Organization and Behavior

We know relatively little about the social system of this greatest of whales. Like all baleen whales, blue whales do not seem very gregari-ous. They are often seen alone, or in small groups, and associations between individuals are short-lived. However, we must be very cau-tious in characterizing the social behavior of this animal as somewhat solitary, for one very good reason: the blue whale has the most pow-erful, and the deepest, voice in the animal kingdom. Vocalizing at frequencies far below our range of hearing (down to as low as 10 Hz), blue whales boom: a typical vocalization is at 180 decibels. What is remarkable about this, other than the sheer power of a blue whale's voice, is that such loud, low-frequency sounds are known to travel in deep water over literally hundreds or even thousands of miles. Recently, scientists have gained access to the formerly secret U.S. Navy

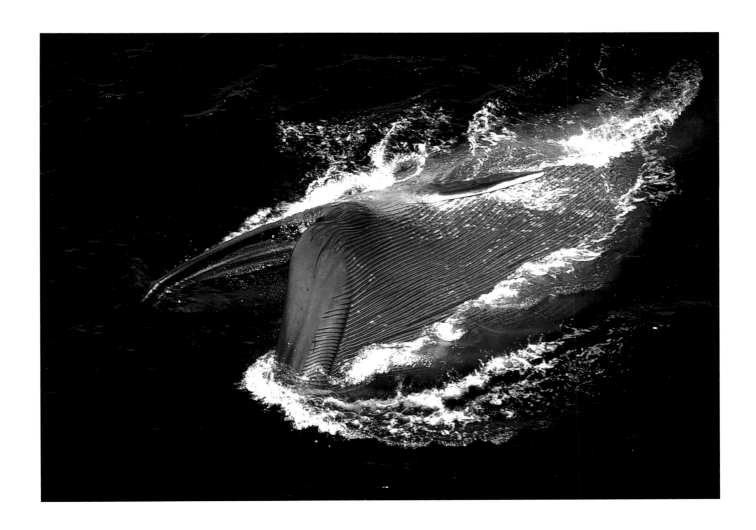

In a remarkable display of power and speed, a blue whale lunges into a school of krill. The huge ventral pouch inflates to engulf tons of water and prey. The largest blue whales probably consume between 6 and 8 tons of food every day during the summer feeding season in high latitudes. Although krill is currently superabundant in the world's oceans, the blue whale's near-total dependence on this prey resource might well make it more vulnerable than many other whale species to massive ecosystem changes.

Like a huge torpedo, a blue whale glides through calm waters. Hydrodynamically perfect, blue whales can probably attain speeds in excess of 20 knots, a characteristic that kept them out of the reach of whalers for centuries. This immunity was brought to an abrupt end by the introduction into whaling of the steam engine, the explosive harpoon and the compressor.

underwater listening network that was originally designed for detecting Soviet submarines (which also make low-frequency sounds). Using this system, individual blue whales have been tracked for many days, and some have been heard from more than 1500 miles (2500 km) away.

Do blue whales actually communicate over these huge distances, as suggested many years ago by Dr Roger Payne? It seems unlikely that one blue whale would want to 'talk' to another across an entire ocean basin, and for me it is hard to see an adaptive purpose behind such truly long-distance communication (over tens of miles, perhaps; but thousands no). An alternative explanation for these sounds has been offered by Dr Chris Clark, who has conducted much of the work with the U.S. Navy system. Clark believes that blue whales are doing something equally remarkable with these great bellows: imaging underwater features from hundreds of miles away as a means of mapping and navigating the oceans. The idea is that a low-frequency sound bounces off something (say, an island or a seamount), and from the reflected echo the whale can determine its location from even a great distance. It is an astonishing suggestion, and not yet proven; but no longer implausible.

Nonetheless, although blue whales may not communicate across oceans, it is quite possible that they do so over shorter distances of tens of miles or more. Hence our caveat about social structure. When we see two blue whales that are several miles apart, we assume they are solitary and not part of a group. Yet such a concept may be meaningless to an animal capable of maintaining group integrity and cohesion over distances that are inconceivable for us. We may yet find a higher-order social system in these animals, but much more research is required.

The mating system of the blue whale is largely unknown. Mating has never been observed, and, perhaps because of their powers of communication, they do not seem to congregate on a breeding ground in the manner of some other species. On rare occasions, scientists have observed what seems to be 'chasing' among blue whales, but the significance and behavioral context of this activity is unknown. As with all baleen whales, our inability to determine the sex of a whale in the field has greatly hampered our understanding of blue whale behavior, although new insights will come shortly from genetic studies.

Catch History and Conservation Status

For hundreds of years, the speed of the blue whale kept this greatest of prizes out of reach of the whalers. All of this changed with the invention of the explosive harpoon, the steam engine and the compressor (the latter being used to inflate a blue whale carcass, which would otherwise sink). As if making up for lost time, the whaling industry last century slaughtered blue whales in unprecedented numbers, particularly in the rich whaling grounds of the Southern Ocean. In the 1930s, more than 150,000 blue whales were killed in the Antarctic. In all, about 360,000 blue whales were killed in the 1900s in the southern hemisphere alone, and many more were taken elsewhere.

We do not know how many blue whales existed prior to the onset of mechanized whaling. However, we do know that whalers came frighteningly close to wiping out this largest and most magnificent of animals. It is likely that more than 95% of the Southern Ocean population was destroyed, and today there are grave concerns for the future of those animals that remain. In the northern hemisphere, some areas in which blue whales were once abundant are now virtually devoid of sightings of this species; these include the Aleutian Islands and northern Norway. While one cannot discount the possibility of a natural change in the distribution of the populations concerned, depletion from overhunting seems a more likely explanation. A mechanized Japanese fishery which began at the turn of the 20th century seems to have all but wiped out blue whales from the Japanese coast and adjacent waters.

Blue whales are now rare almost everywhere, and most biologists consider them to be among the most endangered of the great whales. There is one known exception. A population in the eastern North Pacific off California appears to be large and healthy; its size was recently estimated by Dr Jay Barlow and John Calambokidis at approximately 2000 animals, with a strong growth rate evident. Good news in an otherwise dismal state of affairs.

Fin Whale

Scientific name: *Balaenoptera physalus* ('winged whale' + 'bellows'. The latter is either a reference to the whale's pleated underside, or perhaps to the great blow).

Other common names: finback, finner, razorback, common rorqual.

Maximum size: 89 ft (27 m). Females about 3–10 ft (1–3 m) longer than males.

Distribution: all oceans.

General Characteristics

The fin whale is in some ways as much a mystery today as it was in Herman Melville's time, when the speed of this fastest of whales was still proof against the predations of whaling. 'Let him go,' says Melville. 'I know little more of him, nor does anybody else.'

The second largest animal in our planet's history after the blue whale, the fin whale is truly a giant, reaching lengths of almost 90 ft (27 m) and weights exceeding 140 tons. Long, sleek and hydrodynamically perfect, fin whales are a glorious creation of Nature. They are built for speed, and have been called the 'greyhounds of the ocean'.

Dark gray above and white below, finbacks possess a rare characteristic among mammals in that they are asymmetrically pigmented. If we look at a finback head-on, we are confronted with the unusual sight of a lower jaw that is bright white on one side (the whale's right) but black on the other. The function of this asymmetry is unknown, although the most popular explanation relates to feeding behavior. Since finbacks are often observed circling schools of fish, it has been suggested that a clockwise encirclement will show the bright white of the right lower jaw to the prey, startling them and causing them to pack together more tightly, making it easier for the whale to engulf the entire school. By contrast, a counter-clockwise encirclement would present the black left lower jaw, which would act to camouflage the whale's approach in the underwater gloom (although it is hard to imagine how fish could miss an 80-ft (20-m) animal sneaking up on them!) Other suggestions include a role in social behavior, but ultimately we do not know the answer to this puzzling question.

Swirls of pigment on the right side of the head, known as the 'blaze', and a V-shaped feature across the back behind the blowholes, the 'chevron', contain enough variations between whales that scientists have used these characteristics to identify individuals. The dorsal fin also varies in shape and size, but is generally high and falcate. Behind this feature lies the ridge of the caudal peduncle (tail stock), the sharply defined edge of which gave the fin whale one of its alternative names, the 'razorback'. There are up to about a hundred pleats on the fin whale's underside, and between 260 and 450 plates of baleen on each side of the mouth. The asymmetry already noted is also apparent in the color of the baleen, which is black or dark olive on the left side of the mouth, and white or cream-colored on the right.

Fin whales very rarely raise their tails before a dive. After several blows, the back arches, and the animal submerges in one long, rolling movement. As would be expected from such a powerful whale, the blow is very tall; columnar in shape, it can rise 30–50 ft (10–15 m) into the air on a calm day.

Distribution and Movements

Finbacks are found all over the world, in coastal and shelf waters, and also far out to sea in the pelagic realm. Their migratory behavior appears to be complex, and is not well understood. They exhibit the usual pattern of feeding in high latitudes during summer, and movement to warm waters in winter to breed and give birth, but it is not clear whether all of the population engages in this migration every year. Specific breeding grounds have not been located, and it seems that, like the blue whale, finbacks disperse rather than congregate during winter. There is evidence that the population is sometimes structured by size, with older animals and juveniles segregating into different areas, but this is not a universal pattern. Data from whaling in the northern hemisphere have also suggested that some fin whale populations move latitudinally, with one group moving south in winter to occupy the summer range of another population (which migrates elsewhere at this time). A population in the Mediterranean Sea appears to be non-migratory, and recent genetic analysis by Dr Martine Bérubé suggests that these animals are relatively isolated from finbacks in the nearby North Atlantic.

Where fin whales are born is something of a mystery. It has been assumed that births occur in subtropical or tropical waters, but there is evidence that some births may take place offshore in temperate latitudes. We know from identifying individuals that fin whales return to the same feeding grounds year after year; in the Gulf of Maine, some distinctively marked animals have been observed for 15 years or more. This fidelity to a particular area is maternally directed: a whale will return each spring to the feeding ground to which it was brought during its natal year by its mother.

Life History

At birth, a fin whale calf is enormous by any standard except that of a blue whale. Initially about 21 ft (6.5 m) in length and perhaps 2 tons in weight, a calf grows rapidly and remains with its mother until it is weaned at about seven months. Gestation is 11–12 months. Like the blue whale, the fetal growth rate of a finback includes an astonishing spurt towards the end of pregnancy: the fetus doubles in size during the last two months. Overall, the fetal growth rate of fin and blue whales is the fastest in the animal kingdom, being some twenty times that of primates like humans. Breeding is strongly seasonal, with most births occurring in winter.

Sexually mature at five or six years, a female fin whale will produce calves every two or three years throughout her life. Interestingly, there is evidence that fin whales do not stop reproducing as they reach old age. If we look at levels of pollutants in female mammals, we generally find an increasing burden until the animal begins to reproduce, at which point the contaminants are offloaded to the offspring through the milk. Thus the mother's pollutant burden drops during her reproductive years, and then rises again as she reaches an advanced age and bears no more young. In female fin whales, however, this contaminant level remains constant, suggesting continued reproduction. There is in fact a reliable record of a pregnant finback in her sixties.

Age determination in dead fin whales is fairly straightforward. As in some other rorquals, fin whales have a laminar plug in their ear canal which grows at the rate of two latitudinal layers every year (the ear plug, incidentally, appears to aid, rather than impede, hearing). Thus, one can determine the age of a dead finback by removing this plug, counting the layers and dividing by two. It is clear from this technique that fin whales are long-lived: Dr Alex Aguilar and Dr Christina Lockyer have aged many fin whales, and included among them was a female estimated to be 80 years old.

Diet

The diet of a fin whale is quite variable. Unlike blue whales, they are not confined to krill, although this is a favorite food and is the primary prey of finbacks in the Antarctic. However, they also eat a variety of small schooling fish, including herring, anchovy, capelin and sand lance. Whether fin whales do indeed employ their oddly asymmetric coloration when hunting is not clear, but speed is certainly a principal feature of prey capture. Their supremely sleek bodies and powerful tails are built for speed, and it is likely that they can attain bursts of 25 knots (46 kph) or more when accelerating into schools of fish. Lunging into prey with its huge mouth wide open and its ventral pleats expanded, a fin whale will engulf a vast quantity – many tons – of water and prey. To appreciate the power involved, imagine trying to drag a bucket the size of a finback's mouth through the water at high speed – not an easy task! A fin whale's daily intake of food is exceeded only by that of the blue whale, and may reach 6 tons in the largest animals.

*Hundreds of small fish explode into the air as two fin whales, with studied
coordination, lunge into a prey school at high speed. Note the characteristically black
left lower jaw on both animals; by contrast, the right side is white. This asymmetry, which is very
unusual in mammals, may be related to feeding strategies or to social cues.*

The sleek head of a fin whale barely disturbs the water as it surfaces to breathe. Note the white right lower jaw (contrast with the photo on the previous page), and the large splashguard in front of the blowholes.

Social Organization and Behavior

Like blue whales, finbacks have deep, loud voices that can be heard over great distances underwater. It is possible that, as may also be the case for blue whales, they navigate by bouncing some of these low-frequency booms off islands and other hydrographic features from tens or hundreds of miles away. Whatever the case, fin whales respond to other fin whales at distances of at least several miles, as has been shown when finbacks will move into an area in response to vocalizations made by others who are feeding; whether this constitutes a case of one whale actively advertizing the presence of food to others is not clear.

Melville characterized the social behavior of the fin whale as the cetacean equivalent of misanthropic: 'Very shy; always going solitary.' It is true that fin whales frequently seem to travel alone, although once again we must pause to entertain the possibility that animals separated by considerable distances may be in acoustic contact and therefore are actually part of a highly dispersed group. Social behavior appears to vary by area. In the Gulf of Maine, groups of more than two or three animals traveling side by side are rare. In the Gulf of St Lawrence, however, it is not uncommon to see 10 or 15 animals swimming together. We do not know whether this is due to dissimilar prey between areas requiring different feeding strategies, or to differences in the age composition, and therefore social structure, of the population.

Despite their obvious differences in morphology and coloration, fin and blue whales are closely related. Quite how closely became apparent some years ago when the Icelandic whaling industry killed an animal that was an obvious hybrid between the two species, with characteristics of both. A hybrid is not in itself remarkable, and perhaps not even unexpected given that finbacks are occasionally seen to associate and travel with blue whales; several such hybrids had been reported previously. What was unusual in this case was that the hybrid, a female, was pregnant. It is not known whether the fetus (which genetic analysis showed had been fathered by a blue whale) would have survived to term. Nonetheless, this confuses the issue of how to define a species, since classical biology states that animals of different species cannot interbreed to produce fertile offspring.

How fin whales select mates is a complete mystery. In late autumn in the Gulf of Maine, we have observed tantalizing glimpses of 'chase' behavior by fin whales, and it is possible that this is related to competition among males for access to females. But nothing is known with certainty. No breeding grounds have been identified, copulation has never been observed, and in many ways we know as little about the fin whale's mating system as Melville did a century and half ago. It is likely that genetic analysis of social structure will soon give us some of the first insights into the behavior of this mysterious and beautiful giant.

Catch History and Conservation Status

'There is no means known to catch the fin whale,' lamented Melville in 1851, further noting that the species was 'gifted with such wondrous power and velocity in swimming, as to defy all present pursuit from man.'

Shortly afterwards, however, the 'means' became available in the form of the steam engine and the explosive harpoon, and the fin whale's historic immunity to whaling came to an abrupt end. In terms of sheer numbers killed, fin whales were the favorite prey of 20th-century whalers. In the southern hemisphere alone, an astonishing three-quarters of a million were slaughtered, almost half of these in a single decade, the 1950s. Fin whales were hunted in the North Atlantic as late as 1987, and the remaining whaling nations make no secret of their desire to resume catches of this valuable species.

The status of fin whale populations today is uncertain. In many regions, the fin whale seems to be abundant despite extensive whaling in the past, although we have little idea of how large most current populations are relative to their original sizes. The Antarctic stocks, which bore the brunt of the slaughter, have certainly been greatly diminished. While few scientists would suggest that the fin whale is as endangered in the Southern Ocean as the blue whale, too little is currently known to state that the recovery of these once-great populations is assured.

Sei Whale

Scientific name:	*Balaenoptera borealis* ('winged whale' + 'northern').
Other common names:	Rudolphi's rorqual.
Maximum size:	64 ft (21 m). Females about 3–6 ft (1–2 m) larger than males.
Distribution:	all oceans.

General Characteristics

The name 'sei' comes from the Norwegian word *seje*, meaning pollack or coalfish, on which sei whales have been known to feed. There is much dispute about whether it is pronounced 'sigh' or 'say', but since Norwegians say 'sigh', it seems churlish to adopt any other pronunciation.

Sei whales are fast rorquals that look rather like scaled-down fin whales. In appearance, they closely resemble Bryde's whales, but lack the three rostral ridges which are characteristic of the latter. For many years, this similarity caused whalers to confuse the two species in their catch reports, and in the 19th century (when the fast rorquals were rarely taken at all), any reasonably large dark gray animal was reported as a 'finback'. Sei whales differ from fin whales in having a highly falcate dorsal fin that is stepped further forward on the back, and they lack the white right lower jaw that is the finback's diagnostic feature. Unlike fin whales, they have a tendency to not 'round out' (arch their backs) as they dive. Seis frequently have round pitted scars on their bodies, which apparently originate in bites from the small cookie-cutter shark (*Isistius brasiliensis*) that inhabits warm-water areas within the sei whale's range.

The baleen plates of this species, up to 400 per side and black in color, are rather different from those of the other rorquals in that the fringe of hair on the inner surface is very fine. This is because, unlike the other five species in the family Balaenopteridae, sei whales regularly feed on copepods, and thus require a much finer-mesh straining mechanism to successfully capture these tiny organisms. In this regard the baleen fringes resemble those of right whales (another copepod feeder), although the baleen itself is considerably longer in the latter species. Being rorquals, sei whales have ventral pleats, between 30 and 60 in number.

Distribution and Movements

Sei whales feed in cold water during summer, although they generally do not penetrate as far into high latitudes as fin and blue whales. Presumably their winter distribution is dispersed in offshore waters, and sightings in subtropical and tropical waters at this time indicate that this species migrates to warm water like most other mysticetes.

The sei whale's population structure is not entirely understood, but whaling data give us some clues. Evidence from marked whales (animals into which numbered cylinders had been fired, some of which were later recovered when the whale was killed during whaling operations; see the chapter entitled Whale Research, p117) suggests the existence of at least three populations in the North Pacific, and further that sei whales off California migrate to the area off Vancouver Island, Canada. In the North Atlantic, a migration between the waters off northwestern Africa (a possible winter breeding area) and northern Europe is indicated by whaling data. On the western side of the North Atlantic, data from mark recoveries and the seasonal timing of catches suggests that two populations exist. One population summers off Nova Scotia, while a second occupies the area between Newfoundland and Greenland. In the Southern Ocean, it seems likely that a number of populations exist which inhabit the waters surrounding the Antarctic continent; the degree of exchange among them is not clear, but they presumably migrate northward in winter to warm water areas of the Atlantic, Indian and Pacific Oceans.

In some places (for example, South Africa), information from whaling catches has suggested that the migration of sei whales is loosely segregated by sex, age or reproductive condition. This phenomenon has also been observed in some other whales (notably humpbacks), and presumably relates to individual mating strategies or energy needs.

The most striking feature of the sei whale's movements is its habit of appearing suddenly in an area for days or even months, then disappearing completely for years at a time. My own study area in the Gulf of Maine presents a good example of this. Up until 1986, we had observed only one sei whale in the Massachusetts Bay region in more than ten years. In the summer of 1986, an influx of more than 50 sei whales occurred in the area. The whales remained for several weeks, apparently feeding on unusually high summer concentrations of the copepod *Calanus finmarchicus*. In early autumn, the sei whales disappeared as suddenly as they had arrived. Just two were seen in the area the following year, and none thereafter. This strange phenomenon has also been documented elsewhere, in areas as far apart as Norway, California and Japan. It is presumably caused by opportunistic exploitation of locally abundant prey resources, although why other whales do not make similarly unpredictable movements is unknown.

That sei whales can move over great distances at relatively high speeds is indicated by the record of an animal marked in the Antarctic and killed just ten days later. During the time between marking and recovery, the whale had moved more than 2200 miles (4000 km) – a feat which it must have accomplished at an average sustained speed of almost 10 knots.

Life History and Diet

Newborn sei whale calves are approximately 14 ft (4.5 m) long, and are born in winter after a gestation period of about a year. Sexual maturity is reached sometime between the ages of 6 and 12 years (the best estimate is 10), and females calve at two- to three-year intervals. Ear plug data (see the section on fin whales' life history, p.48) from the Antarctic indicate that sei whales can live for more than 70 years.

There has been much discussion of an apparent decrease in the age at sexual maturity among sei, fin and minke whales in the southern hemisphere. This has been linked to the massive overhunting of many baleen whale species, the idea being that removing so many predators from the region resulted in more food being available for the survivors, who grew and matured faster as a result. However, there are many methodological problems with the data involved. There is good evidence that this phenomenon has occurred among Antarctic minke whales, but the data for both sei and fin whales is rather more problematic.

Sei whales are the most versatile of the rorquals in their feeding habits. In addition to copepods, they also eat krill, various small schooling fish, and even some squid. Much of their foraging involves gulp feeding. However, when eating copepods, sei whales also skim feed like a right whale, and are the only rorqual to employ this behavior.

Social Organization and Behavior

Little is known about the basis of social organization in sei whales. Like most rorquals, they are often seen alone or in small groups, with larger aggregations probably drawn to an area by a common source of food. Nothing is known about the mating system.

Catch History and Conservation Status

Since the sei whale is probably the only rorqual that can rival the fin whale for speed, and is less coastal in its habits, it is not surprising that these animals were left alone by whalers until the 20th century. Even after the introduction of fully mechanized whaling and the opening of the Antarctic grounds, sei whales were taken in only relatively small numbers. However, the decline of larger species, notably the fin and blue whale, found whalers seeking smaller targets, and the sei whale was next in line. Almost 200,000 were killed in the southern hemisphere, with lesser but still substantial numbers taken north of the equator. In some cases, it is difficult to determine the exact numbers because of the frequent confusion with Bryde's whales.

The present status of the sei whale is not well known. Although most populations were depleted by whaling, notably in the Southern Ocean, sei whales are clearly not among the most endangered of whales, and their versatile feeding habits are probably a major factor in their recovery. However, the current abundance of this unpredictably distributed whale cannot be reliably estimated.

Fast and streamlined, a sei whale cruises through clear water. The underside and flanks of this animal carry the small pitted scars that are characteristic of this species, and which probably result from the bites of 'cookie-cutter' sharks or lampreys.

A Bryde's whale arches its back as it 'rounds out' for a sounding dive. Bryde's whales represent a sharp contrast to other mysticetes in that many populations probably never leave warm water, and some appear to breed year-round. Recent DNA analysis has shown that Bryde's whales comprise at least two separate species.

Bryde's Whale

Scientific name: *Balaenoptera edeni* ('winged whale' + edeni, named after Ashley Eden, who was Chief Commissioner of Burma and who provided the type specimen with which this species was described).

Other common names: none.

Maximum length: 51 ft (15.6 m). Females are larger than males, but usually by only a meter or less. A pygmy form is now recognized, and is one or two meters shorter than the 'regular' Bryde's whale.

Distribution: tropical and warm temperate waters worldwide.

General Characteristics

The Bryde's whale suffers the indignity of having been named after a Norwegian named Johan Bryde who initiated a whaling operation in South Africa; the name is pronounced 'BROO-da' (not 'bride'). The Bryde's whale is an excellent example of the confusion that molecular genetic studies have recently injected into traditional taxonomic classifications of animals. Work by Dr Andy Dizon and colleagues has provided strong evidence that the Bryde's whale is not a single species, but at least two. Comparisons of the DNA sequences of two morphologically different forms of Bryde's whales have shown that they are genetically more distant from each other than either is from the sei whale!

In one sense, this is not unexpected. The existence of the two forms, a 'regular' and a 'pygmy', has been known for some years, but the extent of their apparent genetic separation is somewhat surprising. There seems little doubt that the Bryde's whale will soon be split into two species. However, the issue is further complicated by two additional issues. First, the regular form clearly consists of an 'inshore' and 'offshore' type. The marked differences between these two forms in breeding and general ecology (see below) suggest that they may also constitute separate species. Second, the type specimen for *Balaenoptera edeni* is probably the pygmy form, which means that a new name must be assigned to the 'regular' Bryde's whale.

Both forms of Bryde's whales are alike in general appearance, and both resemble the somewhat larger sei whale – a similarity which, as noted earlier, frequently caused whalers to confuse them. At sea, the only practical means of distinguishing these species is to look for the three prominent ridges that run longitudinally down the rostrum of the Bryde's whale, a feature which is absent in the sei and, to make matters worse, is also reported to be missing in some Bryde's whales! Like sei whales, the Bryde's whale is a sleek animal, dark gray above and light-colored below. It has a prominent and highly falcate dorsal fin. There are about 45 ventral pleats, and between 230 and 370 plates of baleen on each side of the mouth. The baleen is slate-gray in color.

Distribution and Movements

The Bryde's whale is the only baleen whale that spends much or all of the year in warm water. It is rarely found above latitudes 30–40°, and then only in areas dominated by warm currents. The larger 'regular' form is itself composed of at least two types which differ in distribution, movements and ecology. Work by Dr Peter Best off South Africa has shown the existence of an inshore form, which is typically found closer to the coast; this animal appears to remain in tropical or subtropical waters year-round, and undertakes only very limited seasonal movements. By contrast, an offshore form is found further from land, and appears to migrate from tropical waters in winter to warm temperate waters in summer. Both forms are found within a latitudinal band in both hemispheres and around the world. The range of the pygmy form is not clear. Current information suggests that it is confined to Australasia, the northern Indian Ocean and areas of southeast Asia, but further research is required.

Life History

Significant differences exist in the ecology and life history of the inshore and offshore forms of the Bryde's whale. The former is unique in being the only baleen whale that breeds year-round rather than seasonally. This is presumably because, having evolved to survive in tropical waters that provide a year-round food supply, the animal has been freed from the constraints of migration. The offshore form, by contrast, is a seasonal breeder. This major difference in reproductive biology suggests (at least to me) that the two forms are probably separate species, but this issue remains unresolved.

Gestation is assumed to be 12 months in all Bryde's whales, and estimates of the age at sexual maturity have ranged from 7 to 13 years (most scientists give a figure of 9–10). Calves of the regular form are probably somewhat less than 13 ft (4 m) long at birth, and are thought to be weaned at about 6 months of age. Females calve every two years. Data from ear plugs (see the section on fin whales, p.48) indicates that Bryde's whales live to at least 55 years.

Diet

Whaling data from South Africa indicate that the inshore form of the Bryde's whale feeds primarily on schooling fish, including anchovies and pilchards. Although the offshore form also takes fish, it seems to subsist primarily on euphausiids (krill). However, it is not known whether these dietary differences occur in other populations of the two forms. Little is known about the diet of the pygmy Bryde's whale, although the stomachs of a few specimens killed in Australian waters contained primarily fish.

Bryde's whales will often roll onto their sides while feeding. They have also been reported to change direction and accelerate rapidly in their pursuit of prey, a behavior which brings to mind feeding dolphins rather than large whales.

Social Organization and Behavior

Very little is known about the social structure of Bryde's whales. Since there appear to be pronounced ecological and reproductive differences between the inshore and offshore forms, it is not unlikely that their social organization and mating system also differ. Existing information suggests the familiar baleen whale pattern of solitary animals or small groups, and occasionally large aggregations, presumably drawn to an area by the presence of food. Beyond this, however, the social life of these animals is largely a mystery.

Catch History and Conservation Status

Bryde's whale was not recognized as a separate species until 1878, and considerable confusion existed about this animal long after that. As a result, the tendency for whalers to misidentify Bryde's whales as other rorqual species has greatly confused the catch statistics for certain areas. It is quite likely that a lot of whales killed in tropical waters and reported as 'finbacks' (particularly during the early part of the 20th century) were Bryde's whales, and there is no doubt that many 'sei whale' catches were actually of this species. As a result, it is not possible to say quite how many Bryde's whales have been killed over the last hundred years.

Bryde's whales have been hunted for centuries in Japanese coastal waters, and they are occasionally taken by an aboriginal whaling operation on the island of Solor in Indonesia. In the 1900s, approximately 20,000 were killed by coastal and high seas whaling operations, with the majority taken in either the southern hemisphere or in Japanese waters. However, the Bryde's whale has never suffered the broad overexploitation that occurred with other large whales; indeed, it was rarely taken before 1920, and some populations have been virtually untouched by hunting. There are no good estimates of abundance for any form of this (these) species, but there is little reason to believe that Bryde's whales are critically endangered anywhere within their range.

(top) The head of a Bryde's whale shows the rostral ridges that distinguish this species from the closely related sei whale.
(bottom) A Bryde's whale lunges on its side into a school of prey.

Minke Whale

Scientific name: Recently divided into two species. Northern hemisphere minkes are *Balaenoptera acutorostrata* ('winged whale' + 'sharp snout') while Antarctic minkes are *Balaenoptera bonaerensis* (+ 'Buenos Aires').

Other common names: little piked whale, lesser rorqual.

Maximum length: 35 ft (10.7 m). Females slightly larger than males.

Distribution: all oceans.

General Characteristics

Given that the minke whale is today the principal target of the whaling industry, its name is something of a sad irony. There is a story that the whale was called Minke's whale after a Norwegian who signed on as crew to a whale catcher in the late 19th century. Being inexperienced, Minke excitedly called out a whale sighting, which proved to be a species of whale which was then considered much too small to be worth the effort of killing. Somewhat derisively, the crew referred thereafter to these animals as 'Minke's whales', and in time the animal picked up the name.

Minkes are frequently referred to as the smallest baleen whale, yet this honor actually goes to the pygmy right whale which, at a maximum length of 20 or 22 ft (6 or 7 m), is smaller still. At 32 ft (10 m) and perhaps 15 tons, a minke is a huge animal when compared to the vast majority of creatures on Earth, but in the company of other great whales it seems almost diminutive.

Minkes are sleek whales that are undoubtedly fast swimmers. They are black or dark gray in color, and the flippers have a prominent white band, although this feature is missing in some populations.

The mouth contains up to about 360 plates of white or off-white baleen. The second part of the minke's scientific name reflects its very pointed head, the tip of which occasionally breaks the surface as the animal rises to breathe. There is rarely a visible blow.

Like the Bryde's whale, the many populations of animals that are all called 'minke whale' are currently the subject of considerable debate regarding taxonomic status. DNA analyses have shown that minke whales in the northern hemisphere are remarkably distant in genetic terms from those in the Antarctic, leading to their separation into two species. Similarly, a dwarf form of the minke whale in the southern hemisphere will probably be given separate species status in the near future.

Distribution and Movements

Given that minkes were not, until fairly recently, a major target for whalers, and also that individuals cannot be reliably identified from natural markings (except in small local populations), we know a great deal less about this species than about other baleen whales. They are found feeding in latitudes that range from temperate to polar. That minkes are migratory is not doubted; but whether all segments of the population undertake these seasonal movements is not clear. There is strong evidence that minke populations on the feeding grounds are segregated by sex, age or reproductive condition. Calves are rarely observed in most areas, and it has been suggested that females wean their young before they return to their summer feeding grounds. However, the exact pattern of movement and population division is not currently known. There is evidence that some areas may host minke whales year-round.

The division (for the purposes of whaling management) of minke whale populations into three oceanic groups – Antarctic, North Pacific and North Atlantic – undoubtedly oversimplifies the true situation concerning population division in this (or these) species. We have learned with other whale species that oceanic populations rarely constitute a single unit, but rather that an ocean basin will contain two or more subpopulations with varying degrees of exchange between them. It is unlikely that minke whales are any different, particularly since certain minke populations show striking evidence of structure that is not observed in other species. However, it remains for genetic analysis to sort out the true story.

Although it is known that minkes occur in low latitudes in winter, specific breeding grounds for this species have yet to be identified. However, recent data from acoustic surveys in the North Atlantic have revealed 'waves' of minkes passing in a broad movement from the east that takes them north of the West Indies, through deep waters offshore of the island chain. This probably reflects a predictable seasonal migration by a segment of the population; whether minkes actually mate and calve at this time is not clear, although there have been a few sightings of young calves in this region.

In the waters of Washington state, biologist Eleanor Dorsey found that a small population of minke whales had individually adjoining ranges, small areas where each animal could be consistently found. The function of these is unclear. Given that territoriality is unknown in baleen whales – and in fact large-scale movements are common even during summer – this is a surprising finding.

Life History and Diet

Newborn minke whale calves average about 8 ft (2.5 m) in length, and are born after a gestation period of 10–11 months. Calves appear to be weaned early, perhaps by the age of five months, and this may explain why they are so rarely observed with their mothers in high latitudes. Sexual maturity is reached at seven or eight years, and females probably calve every other year. Life expectancy is unknown.

The diet of this species is among the most catholic of all whales. Schooling fish of several species, krill and even copepods are consumed; as with most mysticetes, krill is the predominant prey in southern hemisphere populations.

Social Organization and Behavior

Minkes exhibit the typical mysticete pattern of appearing alone, in small groups or within aggregations of seemingly unassociated animals. In some areas, such as the Gulf of Maine, it is extremely rare to see more than one minke traveling side by side but we do not know whether this

is because the population in question is made up primarily of one sex or age class. We know little about the basis of the social system, and essentially nothing about the species' mating habits.

Minkes occasionally breach (interestingly, this behavior is observed quite frequently in some areas, and almost never in others). They are frequently curious enough to approach vessels, a habit which has sometimes had terminal consequences in areas where whaling is practiced.

Catch History and Conservation Status

As noted above, the minke was once considered too small to hunt, but as the whaling industry depleted stocks of the larger whales, it turned to ever smaller species, and finally began to exploit the lowly minke. A few hundred were taken in the Antarctic in the 1950s, but it was not until the 1970s that they began to represent a large portion of the total catch. More than 115,000 were killed in the southern hemisphere last century, and tens of thousands were slaughtered, primarily by Norway, in the North Atlantic. Norway has recently begun to catch several hundred a year for commercial purposes, and Japan continues to take a few hundred for 'scientific research'. Minkes are also hunted by some aboriginal peoples, notably the Greenlandic Inuit.

Because of the current focus by whalers on this species, there have been various attempts to estimate the size of minke whale populations, particularly those of the northeastern North Atlantic and Antarctic. The latter population is estimated at more than 750,000 animals, and there is little doubt that it is large. However, reliably counting such a small, elusive and abundant whale over an area as vast as the Southern Ocean is an extremely difficult task.

Although there is dispute concerning actual numbers, few scientists doubt that minke whales are generally abundant and should not be a priority species in whale conservation efforts. However, there is renewed pressure to permit extensive commercial whaling on minkes. If this ever happens, careful monitoring of the hunt will be essential, given the whaling industry's propensity for deceptive practices and unreasonable catch quotas.

The sharp outline and falcate dorsal fin of a minke whale cut through the waters off Antarctica.
Among the smallest of the baleen whales, minkes are found throughout the world's oceans. Once scorned by whalers,
they are today the main target of commercial hunts.

Humpback Whale

He is the most gamesome and light-hearted of all the whales, making more gay foam and white water than any other of them.

Herman Melville: *Moby Dick*

Scientific name: *Megaptera novaeangliae* ('big wing' + 'New England'. The former refers to the huge flippers, the latter to the location from which the type specimen came).

Other common names: none.

Maximum size: 59–62 ft (18–19 m) reported, but some scientists question this. Females up to 5 ft (1.5 m) longer than males.

Distribution: all oceans, primarily coastal and shelf waters.

General Characteristics

The humpback whale has become one of the most beloved of all whales in recent years, and is the foundation of a burgeoning whale-watching industry in many places. The natural curiosity of the species often brings it close to boats, delighting their occupants. In whaling days, this curiosity was the death of more than a few humpbacks, and was probably one of the reasons that led a Norwegian naturalist to refer to the species as 'the stupidest of all the whales'.

Although the humpback shares many characteristics with the five other rorqual species, it is sufficiently different to be placed in its own genus. Though rather more rotund than the others, it is far from the bloated-looking creature it is often depicted as. The humpback – which is quite sleek and remarkably graceful underwater – has probably suffered more at the hands of inaccurate illustrators than any other whale.

Nonetheless, this is an odd animal in many respects. The head is covered with bumps called tubercles, each of which contains a single stiff hair rather like a cat's whisker. The function of these odd knobs, which

whalers fancifully called 'stovebolts', is probably sensory in nature. By far the most obvious distinguishing characteristics are the huge flippers; about a third the length of the animal, they are far longer than those of any other cetacean.

The dorsal fin shows more variation in shape and size than in any other whale, ranging from almost absent to high and falcate. The tail is generally raised in the air during a dive; on its underside is a unique pattern of markings that ranges from all white to all black and everything in between. Like a fingerprint, no two tail patterns are alike, and scientists use this feature (as well as variations in dorsal fin shape and in scarring) to identify individual humpbacks. The reliability of the tail pattern as an identifying characteristic has formed the basis of many long-term studies of humpback whales.

The humpback is a moderately large baleen whale. Although lengths up to 61 ft (19 m) have allegedly been recorded, maximum adult sizes in the 46 to 50 ft (14–15 m) range are more common. Since all large whales seem to be long-lived, it is quite possible that historic populations contained larger animals which were removed by whaling.

The baleen plates are generally black, and number between 270 and 400 on each side of the mouth with a coarse inner fringe of hair. Being rorquals, humpbacks have ventral pleats; the number varies among individuals, and ranges between 14 and 35. Barnacles can be found in many places on the whale's body, notably on the edges of the tail and flippers, on the chin and sometimes on the dorsal fin.

Distribution and Movements

A truly cosmopolitan species that is found in all oceans of the world, the humpback is among the most migratory of all whales. Indeed, only the gray whale can rival it in the extent of its seasonal movements across ocean basins. Individual humpbacks, identified by their tail patterns, have been observed to travel as much as 5000 miles (8000 km) between their high-latitude summer feeding grounds and winter mating and calving ranges in tropical waters.

This annual migration is among the most predictable of any whale. Whales arrive on their feeding grounds in spring, and forage over hundreds of miles during the summer. In autumn, they begin the return trip to the tropics, where they are generally found in the waters surrounding islands or offshore reef systems. Like most migratory whales, humpbacks do not eat during the winter months, subsisting instead on reserves of fat built up over the summer feeding season.

The migration is somewhat (though not strictly) staggered, with whales of different sexes and maturational classes tending to leave earlier or later than others. For example, newly pregnant females are among the first to leave the breeding areas, and remain on the feeding grounds longer than other whales. This prolonged residency in high latitudes is driven by a need to pack on weight in preparation for the energetically expensive period of lactation they will support after the calf is born. Similarly, females who have just given birth tend to be among the last whales to leave tropical waters at winter's end. There is increasing evidence that mature males will be resident for longer periods than females in the breeding range, presumably to seek as many mating opportunities as possible. Other data suggest that some females may not migrate at all in some years.

In many populations, humpbacks segregate to specific feeding grounds during summer. In the North Atlantic, for example, humpbacks feed in areas which include the Gulf of Maine, Newfoundland, Labrador, Greenland, Iceland and Norway. Fidelity to a particular region is determined matrilineally, so that a whale will return to its mother's feeding ground in later years. Recent genetic research by Dr Per Palsbøll and colleagues has shown that this fidelity seems to persist over thousands of years, a remarkable finding given the humpback's wide-ranging nature and the lack of barriers to dispersal in the ocean. In winter, whales from all areas of the North Atlantic mix on a common breeding ground among the islands of the West Indies.

In the North Pacific, several subpopulations seem to exist. Some humpbacks feed in Alaska and winter off Hawaii. Others summer off California and breed in Mexican waters. On the western side of the Pacific, humpback whales which feed in the Aleutians migrate to mating and calving areas which include some tropical Japanese islands. However, trans-Pacific migrations by identified individuals have recently been recorded, including one from Hawaii to Japan, and another from Vancouver to Japan and back!

In the southern hemisphere, humpbacks feed in a circumpolar distribution around the Antarctic continent, migrating north in winter to different breeding areas in the South Pacific, South Atlantic and Indian Ocean. A population in the Arabian Sea region is unique in that it remains in tropical waters year-round, supported by unusually high productivity in summer.

Life History
On average, humpback whales begin life at a little over 14 ft (4 m) in length. As with most baleen whales, the gestation is close to a year. Births take place during winter, with a peak of calving in early February in the northern hemisphere and early August in austral populations. Lactation (during which a female humpback will lose up to a third of her body weight) lasts longer than in other rorquals: calves remain with their mothers for most or all of their first year of life. Sexual maturity is reached at about five years. Females calve every two or three years, although annual calving is not uncommon in this species.

As with some other species, dead humpbacks can be aged by examining growth layers in the laminar plugs found inside the ear. There is still some dispute about the growth rate of these layers, but the best information indicates that humpback whales can live to at least 48 years. Since in the 20th century more than 95% of these animals had their lives cut short by whaling, the humpback's normal life expectancy may be a good deal longer than this.

With a mixture of curiosity and wariness, a humpback calf looks down upon the camera in the tropical waters where the young whale was born. Clearly visible in the photo are the tubercles along the lower jaw, the ventral pleats, and the long flippers that set humpbacks apart from all other whales.

Megaptera, *the 'big wing'. Lying on its back, a young humpback raises both of its huge flippers into the air
in a display whose meaning is not well understood. Flippering, where the whale slaps the surface with one or both
pectoral fins, is a common activity in this species and probably serves various functions.*

Diet

The diet of a humpback whale includes euphausiids (krill) and a variety of small schooling fish, particularly herring, sand lance and capelin. Being gulp feeders, they lunge into a prey school with mouths agape, taking in a large quantity of water and food before expelling the water through the baleen. All rorquals do this, of course, but humpbacks are unique in the ingenious methods they use to catch some of their prey, particularly fish. Whales will often blow nets or clouds of bubbles around or below a school of fish. The bubbles somehow trap or concentrate the prey, making it much easier for the whale to engulf as many fish as possible in the final lunge.

Interestingly, this bubble-feeding technique varies not only among individuals, but also between populations. In the North Atlantic, most whales seem to prefer bubble clouds, which involve the release of innumerable bubbles in a single burst that may be as much as 65 ft (20 m) across. A minority of North Atlantic humpbacks employ bubble nets, a more involved technique which requires the whale to swim upwards in a spiral while releasing columns of bubbles at rather precise intervals; the 'net' closes just before the whale makes the lunge. In the North Pacific, bubble clouds have never been recorded, and all whales use either bubble nets or a variety of related structures in their feeding.

Individual whales will often add refinements to the basic feeding technique. These include lobtail or kick feeding, where a humpback will slap the water with its tail at the beginning of a feeding sequence, perhaps to create bubbles or to stun the prey. A few whales even breach before making a feeding lunge.

Social Organization and Behavior

We know a good deal about humpback whale social systems, and will shortly learn a lot more from genetic studies. Like all baleen whales, humpbacks rarely form stable associations, and are usually found alone or in small groups. An individual whale will associate with many other animals during the course of a year, or even a day. Pairs are occasionally seen to remain together for weeks or months, but in most populations this seems to be rare. There is one exception, however. On the Alaskan feeding grounds, scientists have observed a remarkable semi-stable group for a number of years. Although this group gains and loses some members over time, it contains a core of individuals who remain together for long periods. The group does not seem to consist of related animals. It is possible that its cohesion reflects the association of several whales with similar feeding styles who maximize their prey intake by foraging cooperatively.

Just as the humpback whale's year shows a distinct geographic separation between winter and summer, so too does its behavior exhibit marked seasonal contrasts. In summer, whales frequently feed together. At this time, cooperation appears to be the rule, and aggression is almost never observed. In winter, things are very different. Once on the breeding grounds, males will often engage in combat for access to mature females. These spectacular fights take place in 'competitive' groups, which generally consist of a single female and anywhere from two to more than twenty males. One male escorts the female, and attempts to fend off challenges from other males intent on displacing him from his position. Tail slashes, head butting, body slams and charge strikes are common. Competitive groups may remain together for only a few minutes, or for several hours, and they often gain and lose members. Ultimately, they break up, leaving the female with whichever male has succeeded in winning (or retaining) the key position next to her. Whether mating takes place at this time, or has taken place prior to challenges from other males, is unknown. Remarkably, copulation has never been observed in this species; apparently humpbacks confine their amours to the underwater realm.

Direct competition for females is not the only strategy pursued by mature males, and this is where we come to the famous song of the humpback whale. Many animals, from crickets to birds, sing in the biological sense of making sounds in a repeated pattern. In many species, it is the males who do so, generally for the purpose of soliciting females or advertising territory. Humpback whale song is remarkable because of its complexity. Songs are sung only by males, and typically consist of several themes which are sung in a specific order. A song may take from a few minutes to half an hour to complete. Having reached the end, the whale will return to the beginning and repeat the performance. Humpbacks can sing continuously for hours or even days, their haunting voices filling the depths of the ocean for miles around.

Remarkably, humpback songs change progressively over time. Whales in one population, such as the West Indies, will sing the same song, but somehow keep up with slow changes that occur over the course of one, and then several, winters. Which males lead these changes, and why, we do not know, yet over the course of a few years songs become unrecognizably different in form and content. Whales in different populations sing different songs, and they too undergo a slow transformation with which all the singers keep pace.

It is very likely that the main function of song is to attract females, although it may also serve to maintain spacing between males. Although most singing is done in the tropics during winter, song is also heard at times on the feeding grounds. Since whales do not mate during summer, this adds to the mystery of the song's social role.

More than any other whale, the humpback engages in often spectacular aerial behaviors. These include breaching, lobtailing, and flippering. These displays are seen at all times of year and among whales of all ages. They clearly have multiple functions which differ with context; possible explanations include communication, parasite removal, excitement or play.

Catch History and Conservation Status

Being slow and often coastal in its habits, the humpback was frequently one of the first species to be taken whenever shore whalers set up operations in a new area. Humpback oil was considered a poor substitute for that of some other species, notably the sperm whale, and its whalebone (baleen) was of inferior quality to that obtained from bowhead or right whales. Nonetheless, many humpbacks were taken before the advent of mechanized whaling. Whalers from one or two ports actually specialized in 'humpbacking'. In particular, vessels from

Provincetown on Cape Cod were known for their prosecution of this fishery in the West Indies and Cape Verde Islands during the 19th century. In the 1870s, one Provincetown whaler took as crew a fisherman from the tiny Caribbean island of Bequia, and taught him how to catch humpbacks. Some time later, the man returned home and began a small native fishery which persists on Bequia to this day.

Humpbacks were hit particularly hard by modern whaling techniques. Although thousands were killed in the northern hemisphere, the greatest damage occurred on the great whaling grounds of the Southern Ocean, where more than 200,000 were slaughtered last century. Of this number, almost a quarter were taken illegally by the Soviet Union. The Soviets reported killing 2700; the actual number was more than 48,000. Other illegal catches were made in the Antarctic by the factory ship *Olympic Challenger*, owned by Aristotle Onassis.

Overall, it seems likely that most humpback whale populations were reduced by 95% of their original numbers. Today, however, this species is making a strong comeback in many areas. The North Atlantic population was recently estimated at more than 10,000 animals, and it is quite likely that this is an underestimate. In the North Pacific, there is increasing evidence that the population is larger than had been thought, although recent analysis of historic whaling data from California suggests that the eastern stock is still well below its pre-exploitation levels. Data from the southern hemisphere also indicates strong growth in some populations.

The resilience of the humpback whale is probably due to a combination of its relatively high reproductive rate and broad diet. As one who has studied humpbacks for many years, I have little doubt that, given time and a lack of further threats, this remarkable species will make a full recovery in most places. However, although commercial whaling on humpbacks has long since ceased, entanglement in fishing gear and depletion of prey resources by human fisheries may represent a significant problem for some populations. Let us hope that it is not so, and that the humpback's haunting song will not soon be stilled in the great blue realm of the sea.

Northern Right Whale

Scientific name: Recently divided into two species. North Atlantic right whales are *Eubalaena glacialis* ('true whale of the ice') while those in the North Pacific are *Eubalaena japonica* ('true whale of Japan').

Other common names: black right whale, Biscayan right whale, Nordkaper.

Maximum size: 59–60 ft (18 m). Females 3–6 ft (1–2 m) longer than males.

Distribution: North Atlantic and North Pacific (including the Okhotsk Sea), primarily coastal and shelf waters.

General Characteristics

The northern right whale is arguably the world's most endangered great whale. Its physical appearance is often described somewhat euphemistically as 'robust' (the uncharitable would say fat), and it is probably the slowest of all the whales. The right whale is distinguished by its massive black body, lack of a dorsal fin and broad flippers. The huge tail can be as much as 22 ft (7 m) across. It is proportionately the broadest tail of any whale, and is frequently raised before a dive. The blow, when seen from directly ahead or behind, is distinctly V-shaped, a result of the wide separation of the nostrils. Right whales are distinguished from the bowhead by a somewhat smaller head relative to the overall body size, the lack of the bowhead's 'steeple-top' crown below the blowholes, and most noticeably by the presence on the head of numerous rough growths known as callosities.

Callosities are a natural feature of the whale whose function is not well understood. Interestingly, they occur in the same places on the head on which one would find hair in a human: the top of the head (known as the 'bonnet'), upper and lower lips, on the chin and above the eyes. The pattern of callosities is unique to each animal, and is the principal feature used by scientists to recognize individual right whales. Although the callosities are naturally black or gray, they are colonized by millions of parasites called cyamids, or whale lice. These tiny amphipod crustaceans give the callosities on which they reside a yellow or red color, making it much easier for researchers to discern the outline of the callosity. Cyamids eat dead skin, and perhaps also use the whale as a base from which to feed on microscopic organisms in the surrounding water.

There are between 220 and 260 baleen plates on each side of the mouth. Right whale baleen can reach almost 10 ft (3 m). Only bowheads' baleen is longer. Narrow, and black in color, these plates are fringed on their inner surface by silky, luxuriant hair. This serves as a fine-mesh filter with which to trap the tiny zooplankton on which the whale subsists.

Right whales are massive animals, weighing more per foot of body length than any other species except the bowhead, and it is likely that the largest rights reach 100 tons. This species, which is somewhat larger than the southern right whale, provides an apparent exception to the general rule that southern hemisphere baleen whales are larger than their northern hemisphere counterparts.

Distribution and Movements

Because of whaling, the northern right whale's present range represents a considerable contraction from that of the past. Even the original scientific name of the species ('true whale of the ice') is today a sad irony, since right whales have virtually disappeared from the higher-latitude portions of their range, notably in the North Atlantic where they were once found off Greenland, Iceland and northern Norway. Today, the right whale exists in low numbers in the western North Atlantic and western North Pacific, and is extremely rare in the eastern part of either ocean.

Right whales spend much of their lives in coastal waters. Thanks to long-term studies in the western North Atlantic by Dr Scott Kraus, Dr Charles Mayo and colleagues, we know a good deal about the biology of this species. Right whales spend the summer in temperate latitudes such as the Gulf of Maine, where they feed and nurse their young; much of the latter activity takes place in embayments which appear to serve as nursery grounds, among them the Bay of Fundy and Cape Cod Bay. In winter, pregnant females and some other members of the population migrate to warm water off Georgia and Florida, where the females give birth. It is not known where the remaining portions of the population spend the winter, although animals begin to appear in Massachusetts waters as early as late January.

A similar pattern may exist in other populations, although there is evidence from 19th-century whaling logs that North Pacific right whales calved in offshore waters. An occasionally voiced assumption that the west coast of the United States and Mexico was once an important breeding habitat for this species is not supported by either early whaling data or information from archaeological sites in this region. Right whales are occasionally observed off California, Baja California (Mexico), and even Hawaii, but these areas do not appear to have been a significant part of their historic range in the North Pacific.

Life History

Gestation in right whales is a year. Newborn calves measure an average of 15–16 ft (4–5 m) in length, and generally remain with their mothers for the better part of a year. Sexual maturity is reached between 6 and 12 years, and females calve once every three or four years.

We know that right whales are long-lived, in part because of a remarkable chance that occurred recently in the research field. A newspaper photograph from Florida in 1935 featured a distinctively marked female right whale whose calf had been killed by local whalers. Amazingly, scientists from the New England Aquarium in Boston were able to match the photo to another of the same whale taken many years later. This animal was last seen in 1994. Assuming that she was at least 10 years old in 1935 – probable given that she had a calf – she would have been close to 70 when last observed.

Diet

Right whales are true plankton feeders. They are skimmers who move through a patch of plankton with their huge mouths agape, continuously filtering prey as they swim; this is done at depth or, less frequently, at the surface. They eat primarily copepods, organisms about the size of a grain of rice. Thus, right whales are something of a paradox of nature, for here we have one of the largest animals on Earth subsisting on some of the smallest. It is a testament to both their efficiency and to the extraordinary biomass of plankton that the largest of these whales will somehow manage to consume 2 or 3 tons of copepods a day. Other occasional diet items are barnacle larvae and euphausiids.

Since copepods are densely concentrated in patches that may be as much as several miles apart, right whales must be capable of efficiently locating these food resources in often large areas of ocean. Work by Dr Charles Mayo and colleagues off Cape Cod, Massachusetts, has shown that right whales are not only supremely good at finding such patches, but also at foraging within them in such a way that they constantly exploit the highest-density portions of the patch. How they do this is unknown. Victoria Rowntree and David Mattila have both suggested the intriguing (though unproven) idea that, since the whale lice that live on the heads of right whales also eat copepods, the whales may somehow use the behavior and movements of the lice as 'sensors' of copepod density.

Social Organization and Behavior

The social behavior of right whales is fascinating. Although they are seasonal calvers, giving birth largely in mid winter, they appear to engage in sexual activity at all times of year. Thus, unless female right whales store sperm for later fertilization (a phenomenon which is unknown in any cetacean), the only activity leading to conception will take place in winter. It is possible that sexual behavior at other times represents a 'trying out' of males that aids females in mate selection later on.

Mating groups frequently consist of a single female and numerous males, the latter jostling for position within the group. Perhaps the most

A courtship group of northern right whales. On occasion, such groups can consist of more than thirty whales, the majority of which are males jostling for position around a central female (seen here raising her flipper in the air). Females sometimes mate with several males in succession. Although these groups are common in summer, it is unlikely that matings at this time lead to conception.

remarkable aspect of the male right whale is the size of the testes, which at a staggering one ton are the largest in the animal kingdom. To appreciate how extraordinary this is, it is worthwhile to compare the relative testes size of the blue whale, which is the largest animal on earth and in which mature males may be twice as long and twice as heavy as an adult male right whale. In blue whales, the testes weigh only 150 lb (70 kg).

Scientists have theorized that, as occurs in some primates and many other animals, the large testes are associated with a mating system that is heavily dependent upon sperm competition. Large testis size is often found in species where females mate with multiple partners (e.g. chimpanzees), the theory being that the testes produce huge quantities of sperm to compete with that of the female's other mates. This fits well with our observations in this case, since female right whales have been seen to copulate with more than one male in succession.

When not breeding, right whales are found alone or in small loose groups. They generally feed alone, but have occasionally been observed 'echelon feeding', where two or more animals will skim-feed side by side in the same plankton patch. Little is currently known about whether kinship plays any role in social behavior. However, since scientists have succeeded in sampling most members of the western North Atlantic population for genetic studies, it is likely that many questions of this kind will be answered in the near future.

Catch History and Conservation Status

The northern right whale was the first species to be taken by humans on a systematic commercial basis, beginning no later than the 11th century. Details of the hunting and decline of northern right whale populations worldwide are given in the chapter on Whaling, p107. The eastern North Atlantic population was the first to be severely reduced, followed by the western North Atlantic, eastern North Pacific and western North Pacific, in that order.

Today, right whales are critically endangered throughout their range. Not surprisingly given its hunting history, the population in European waters is all but extinct. The right whale was rare in this region by 1800, and the last substantial remnant was probably wiped out by a burst of Norwegian whaling around 1900. The western North Atlantic population numbers fewer than 300 animals, and despite more than six decades of protection shows no sign of recovery. This is undoubtedly due in part to a combination of the slow reproduction of this species (relative to the rorquals) and a heavy toll of human-caused mortalities. Unfortunately, North Atlantic right whales suffer mortalities from entanglements in fishing gear and from ship strikes more than any other large whale.

In the North Pacific, the eastern population is now so small that even a single sighting is reported in the scientific literature. Recent analysis of sighting records from this ocean by myself and Dr Robert Brownell strongly suggests that the eastern North Pacific right whale was a victim of illegal Soviet whaling catches in the 1960s (see the chapter on whaling for further details). In the western North Pacific and Okhotsk Sea, recent sightings suggest that right whales may number in the low hundreds, but too little is known of this population to assess its current status.

We do not know what the future holds for northern right whales, but they are certainly precariously balanced at the edge of a precipice. Rare, slow-breeding and often living in highly developed, highly trafficked coastal waters, everything seems stacked against their survival. An additional question concerns whether the different populations are each so small that they have lost genetic diversity and are thus suffering the effects of inbreeding. Inbreeding can result in the expression of 'bad' genes that in a healthy population would remain recessive, leading to immune deficiency, infertility and other problems. The issue of inbreeding is complex and much debated, and there is little agreement on how much of an impact it can have on a species' recovery. In the case of northern right whales, ongoing genetic research may give us some answers. For now, we must do what we can to protect them and hope that their future is not as bleak as it sometimes appears.

Water falls in graceful sheets off the broad tail of a northern right whale. As in all whales, the powerful tail is the animal's primary unit of propulsion. However, it also serves as a heat exchanger, shedding excess heat by passing warmed blood through an extensive network of capillaries that lie close to the surface.

Southern Right Whale

Scientific name:	*Eubalaena australis* ('true whale' + 'southern').
Other common names:	none.
Maximum length:	about 56 ft (17 m). Females 3–6 ft (1–2 m) longer than males.
Distribution:	southern hemisphere, including South Atlantic, South Pacific, Antarctic and southern Indian Ocean. Primarily coastal and shelf waters, including remote islands.

General Characteristics

The southern right whale is traditionally considered a separate species from its northern counterpart. The basis for this distinction is somewhat questionable, since gene flow is much more likely to occur across the equator in either the Atlantic or Pacific (i.e. between northern and southern right whales in these two oceans) than between the populations of northern right whales that are separated by the North American continent. This taxonomic issue will probably be resolved shortly by molecular genetic studies.

Southern right whales are essentially similar in form to their northern counterparts (see the previous chapter). Like northern right whales, the southern animals are large, rotund and heavy, with huge tails, broad flippers and callosity patterns that are individually distinctive. The northern species appears to be slightly larger overall; this is rather odd since it represents an interesting and unexplained exception to the general rule that southern hemisphere baleen whales are bigger than their boreal counterparts. In addition, some differences in callosity patterns have been noted between the two species.

Southern right whales were the first large whales to be the subject of a long-term study of identified individuals. In 1969, Dr Robert Brownell discovered an important concentration of right whales wintering off Península Valdés, Argentina; the following year, Dr Roger Payne began a study of this population which continues today.

Distribution and Movements

Southern right whales are frequently found in coastal and shelf waters. They occur all around the southern hemisphere, including South America, South Africa, Australia and New Zealand. They also inhabit the Antarctic, as well as coasts of remote mid-oceanic islands such as Kerguelen, Tristan da Cunha and the Crozets. There seems to be little exchange between the various continental populations. To date, photo-identification of individual right whales has not revealed any movements between South America and South Africa, the sites of two long-term studies. However, individuals from Argentinian waters have also been seen off Tristan da Cunha and Bird Island, both of which are in mid ocean, and one whale was seen to move from Gough Island in the central South Atlantic to the South African coast.

So are the two populations separate, or do they ever mix? Here, as with many other cetacean species, modern genetic analysis is helping to clarify the picture. Recent work by Victoria Portway has given support to the idea that Argentinian and South African right whales belong to separate stocks, although it is possible that some individuals occasionally meet 'halfway' off the remote islands of the mid-Atlantic ridge. A similar situation probably prevails between other Southern Ocean populations.

Right whales migrate from temperate or high latitudes in summer to warmer waters in winter, when they calve and probably mate. The migratory movements of individuals from year to year may depend in part on their sex and reproductive condition; for example, there is strong evidence that females travel to different areas depending on whether they are pregnant or not. This is also the case in northern right whales, as is the tendency for females with calves to use specific 'nursery' areas which are often located in bays.

Life History and Diet

No major differences in life history patterns have been reported between this species and the northern right whale; gestation, sexual maturity and calving interval all appear to be similar in the two species. Southern right whales are seasonal breeders which calve in the austral winter. There are no good data on their life expectancy, but there is currently no reason to believe that they are any less long-lived than the northern animals.

The diet is also similar, although it is possible that southern right whales in the Antarctic feed more frequently on krill than the northern right whale does. Copepods appear to be the major prey item for both species.

Social Organization and Behavior

Extensive observations by Dr Roger Payne's group at Península Valdés, Argentina, have documented similar patterns of social and mating behavior to those reported for northern right whales. The huge size of the testes in males is further evidence that the mating system is similar to that of the northern animals, with females sometimes mating with multiple males on one occasion.

In Argentina, Dr Payne's group has found that male right whales have more and larger callosities on their heads than females. In addition, males tend to have more scarring on their bodies. This has been interpreted to mean that males fight over females, using their callosities as weapons to scratch and injure competitors. Fights such as occur in humpback whales, where males exhibit obvious and often spectacular aggression in contests over females, are not seen in right whales; however, aggressive 'jostling' in large courtship groups may be a feature of the mating system of this species.

One behavior that has not been reported for northern right whales is 'sailing', a quite common activity off Argentina. There, right whales will raise their great tails into the air and 'sail' downwind for considerable distances before swimming back upwind and repeating the behavior. Whether this remarkable activity serves some practical purpose, or is instead undertaken purely for the fun of it, is unknown.

Catch History and Conservation Status

Whaling for southern right whales seems to have begun in the late 18th century as a result of American and French efforts to find new sperm whaling grounds. It is clear from contemporary accounts that the species was highly abundant at the onset of this enterprise. One observer, commenting on the profusion of right whales off the islands of St Paul and Amsterdam in the early 1800s, noted that 'what could be said of its abundance would hardly appear credible.'

Dr Peter Best has used American import records for whale oil and baleen to estimate the number of animals taken during the 19th century. His work suggests that almost 60,000 southern right whales were killed by American whalers alone during this period. One estimate gives a total figure of almost 200,000 animals killed in less than twenty years at the beginning of the 19th century. While this seems very high, it is not entirely inconceivable given the number of vessels in the fishery at this time.

As a result of this heavy exploitation, southern right whale populations in many areas were already highly depleted by the time that modern whaling began in the southern hemisphere early in the 20th century. As a naturalist named Bolau noted, now that these 'once so rich fishing grounds are abandoned, the giants of the sea are mostly killed by the war of destruction which man's greed has waged against them without pity'.

Some 8000 right whale catches are recorded from the 20th century, including about 3200 animals that were illegally killed by the Soviet Union long after they had supposedly received international protection. Today, there is no doubt that this species is much better off than the northern right whale. Although reliable estimates are difficult to obtain, it is thought that the southern right whale numbers in the thousands. Despite their catch history, they seem to be rebounding strongly in every population that is currently under study, and there is now considerable hope for their recovery.

*A right whale cruises along at the surface with its mouth open, continuously filtering large
numbers of tiny copepods from the water passing through its mouth. The whale's baleen, the upper
section of which is visible in this photo, extends up to 8 ft (2.4 m) from the jawline. Note also the
callosities on the head; whalers referred fancifully to these as the 'bonnet'.*

Bowhead Whale

Scientific name: *Balaena mysticetus* ('whale' + 'moustached whale').

Other common names: Greenland right whale, great polar whale.

Maximum length: almost 65 ft (20 m). Females about 3 ft (1 m) longer than males.

Distribution: exclusively northern hemisphere, in arctic and sub-arctic areas.

General Characteristics

No other large whale is as completely adapted to life in cold water as the bowhead. Huge and robust, with a blubber layer that can be more than 20 in (50 cm) thick, the bowhead spends much of its year associated with ice. The head, which makes up more than a third of the animal, is triangular in shape and rises to a sharp crown at the blowholes, giving a characteristic peaked appearance which whalers called the 'steepletop'. This huge head can break through ice 6 ft (2 m) thick. The body is black except for the chin area, which is white.

At its maximum recorded length of 65 ft (19.8 m), the bowhead is a massive animal whose weight can probably exceed 100 tons. The mouth is vast, and contains up to about 700 plates of baleen which, at a maximum length of 14 ft (4.5 m), are easily the longest of any mysticete. Like the right whale (to which this species is probably more closely related than its current classification suggests), bowheads have widely separated blowholes, giving them a distinct V-shaped blow. They can be a very difficult animal to follow: bowheads are adapted to swimming long distances under ice, and will sometimes travel for a couple of miles before surfacing, even in ice-free waters. They can dive for rather longer than other baleen whales, remaining underwater for close to an hour in some cases.

Distribution and Movements

Bowheads are found only in the northern hemisphere. Closely associated with sea ice for much of the year, they are the only baleen whale that never migrates to low latitudes. Several populations exist. The largest and best-known inhabits the western Arctic, migrating between the Bering, Beaufort and Chukchi Seas. In the eastern Arctic, three populations are recognized: Hudson Bay/Foxe Basin, Davis Strait/Baffin Bay, and Spitsbergen and the Barents Sea. Another population, probably isolated, inhabits the Okhotsk Sea.

Migrations are restricted and are dependent upon ice. Bowheads are typically found along the southern edge of the pack ice in winter, or in polynyas, and move north as the ice breaks up in spring. Since bowheads have been observed to alter course to swim around icebergs long before they can possibly see them, it has been suggested that the low-frequency 'grunts' made by migrating whales may be a primitive form of echolocation.

Life History and Diet

Bowhead calves are born during the spring migration or in early summer, after a gestation period that may be as long as 13 to 14 months. Calves average about 13–15 ft (4–4.5 m) in length at birth, and are probably weaned some time before the age of a year. Bowheads are slow breeders. Recent data suggest that they may not reach sexual maturity until 15–20 years, and females produce a calf every three or four years thereafter. However, the species may be exceptionally long-lived. In 1993, a large male bowhead killed by the Alaskan Inuit was found to have been carrying in its flesh a stone harpoon point. Since this type of harpoon is not known to have been used after 1900, it suggests that bowhead life expectancy can reach 100 years.

Bowheads primarily eat copepods and euphausiids, but more than sixty species of animals have been found in the stomachs of hunted bowheads. Bowheads feed everywhere from the sea floor to the surface. Like their relatives the right whales, they frequently skim-feed. Huge volumes of water pass through the vast mouth, trapping prey organisms on the fine mesh of hair that lines the interior of the long baleen plates.

Social Organization and Behavior

Like right whales, bowheads frequently travel alone or in small groups, although large aggregations may be found on the feeding grounds. Little is known about social behavior, although as with other mysticetes, stable groups (except for mothers and their calves) seem rare. Mating is assumed to take place in late winter or early spring, but sexual activity has been observed virtually year-round. Like right whales, male bowheads have huge testes, which strongly suggests that sperm competition plays a major role in the mating system of the species. Females are sometimes observed with several male consorts, and may mate with multiple males. Bowheads breach and lobtail, although the function of these displays is unknown. Vocalizations are frequent at certain times of year, and may play a significant role in breeding.

Catch History and Conservation Status

After the northern right whale, it was the bowhead which bore the brunt of medieval commercial whaling. The Basques killed both bowheads and right whales in southern Labrador in the early 16th century. The discovery of innumerable bowheads at Spitsbergen by a prospector for the English Muscovy Company in 1611 unleashed a flood of exploitation. 'At this time,' wrote the great whaling captain and naturalist William Scoresby, 'the mysticetus was found in immense numbers throughout the whole extent of the coast.' Scoresby also noted that the whales knew no fear of humans, and were thus easily captured. By about 1700, the bowhead was scarce in this area, and whalers sought new grounds on which to pursue this most valuable of prey.

In 1719, Dutch whalers began to kill bowheads off West Greenland and in the Davis Strait, and the vessels of other nations soon followed. Before long the entire area, including Baffin Bay and Foxe Basin, was being worked. By 1841, the industry that pursued the Greenland whale, as it was known, was in decline. Although a few bowheads were taken over the next 40 or 50 years, the vast populations that had once stretched from Canada to the Norwegian high Arctic were now fragmented and reduced to a tiny fraction of their original size.

By this time, however, the bowhead's two other great strongholds had been discovered. In 1843, bowheads were discovered in the Okhotsk Sea in such numbers that there were more than three hundred vessels operating there during a single season. Then in 1848, a whaling ship named *Captain Roys* became the first such vessel to pass through the Bering Strait and into the Arctic waters beyond. There, the crew found 'whales innumerable, some of which yielded 280 barrels of oil.' Again, large numbers of whaling ships flocked to the region. As usual, the populations in both areas were soon depleted to the point where whaling ceased to be profitable.

As with northern right whales, most of the damage to bowhead populations had already been done by 1900, and neither species was the target of large-scale whaling this century. However, we now know that the Soviets illegally killed many bowheads in the Okhotsk Sea in the 1950s.

Today, it is largely accepted that the western Arctic bowhead population is recovering slowly; a survey in 1993 estimated its size at 8000 animals and growing. By contrast, recent estimates have put the total population in the eastern Arctic at only a few hundred whales. Of these, there may be about four or five hundred bowheads in the Davis Strait and Hudson Bay populations. The Spitsbergen/Barents Sea stock is rarely observed nowadays and may be close to extinction, although the relationship between the three eastern substocks, and whether exchange occurs among them, is not clearly understood. Even in the more abundant Davis Strait population, the reproductive rate appears to be low. Little is known of the present status of Okhotsk Sea bowheads, but surveys in the region suggest that the population may be in the low hundreds.

Bowheads are still hunted off Alaska by the Inuit, although most biologists accept that this well-managed subsistence fishery has little impact on the growing western Arctic population.

A bowhead in Arctic waters exposes the white chin that is characteristic of this species. The bowhead is well named: the upper jaw is strongly arched, and powerful enough to smash its way through thick ice. Just dissipating at the left edge of the photo is the animal's blow which (as in right whales) is distinctly V-shaped.

Gray Whale

Scientific name: *Eschrichtius robustus* (named after the Danish zoologist Eschricht; robustus = 'strong').

Other common names: none.

Maximum length: 49 ft (15 m). Females about 3 ft (1 m) longer than males.

Distribution: North Pacific only, although recently extinct in the North Atlantic.

General Characteristics

Known to whalers as the 'devil fish' for the ferocity with which it sometimes resisted capture, the gray whale is an odd animal in many ways. Alone in its own taxonomic family, it is different from other baleen whales in its appearance and in some of its habits. However, there is much debate about whether the gray whale really deserves such a separate classification: recent genetics work has suggested, although not proved, that it is quite closely related to the balaenopterid whales (the rorquals).

The gray whale is indeed a mottled gray in color, often with numerous scars and barnacles. There is no dorsal fin as such, but rather a dorsal 'hump' followed by a series of ridges running down the tail stock. Like some other slow whales, grays support a substantial population of cyamids (whale lice) in various places on their bodies. Barnacles are also found in profusion, and it has been said that a large gray whale may carry a load of up to half a ton of these crustacean hitchhikers, who use the whale as a base from which to filter feed on plankton in the surrounding water. The gray whale's mouth contains between 130 and 180 yellowish plates of baleen per side.

Distribution and Movements

Gray whales are migratory animals in the extreme; the only species that can challenge the scope of their seasonal movements is the humpback. Each autumn, they begin a several-thousand-mile journey from their feeding grounds in the north to mating and calving areas in tropical waters; the return migration is made the following spring.

The species is today found only in the North Pacific Ocean. Two populations of the gray whale are recognized, in the eastern and western North Pacific, and they are believed to be largely separate from one another. The eastern population feeds in the northern Bering, southern Chukchi and southwestern Beaufort Seas during the summer months, and calves in winter in shallow lagoons along the Pacific coast of the Baja Peninsula. Some animals appear to end their northward spring migration further south along the coasts of British Columbia and southern Alaska. All in all, this migration is one of the longest undertaken by any mammal, with the most extreme movements covering more than 5000 miles (8000 km).

The western population is less well known. Gray whales from this stock appear to summer in the Sea of Okhotsk, and migrate to the mainland coast of Asia. It has been suggested that breeding grounds may exist along the coast of southern China, but this remains unproven. It is not known whether a reliance on coastal lagoons for calving (as is the case for the eastern population) is a characteristic of this species throughout its range.

One of the most interesting aspects of the gray whale's distribution is that it appears to have been extant in the North Atlantic until very recently. Historical records from Iceland describe a whale, called the 'sand-lier', which sounds very much like a gray whale. New England whalers in the 18th century occasionally hunted what they termed 'scrag whales', which again sound from the descriptions like grays. More convincing yet is the discovery of various gray whales' bones which are estimated to be only two or three hundred years old.

What happened to the North Atlantic gray whale? There are two views on this. The first suggests that, while grays in this ocean may well have been hunted on occasion, whaling records do not give us any indication that the species was taken in sufficient numbers to cause its extinction. It may be that the gray whale was already on its way out as a result of some natural processes, and whaling merely hastened its demise. If, like the California population, the Atlantic gray whale relied on lagoons for calving, perhaps this habitat disappeared, or the animal was forced out by early settlers on both sides of the ocean.

The second view is that, given the extremely coastal habits of this species, it is difficult to imagine early European whalers *not* taking gray whales in substantial numbers, especially given that they are known to have hunted right whales for the same reason. The lack of records of such exploitation is curious (after all, there are good records of the right whale fishery). However, if this hunting occurred prior to records being kept, and was concentrated on highly vulnerable breeding populations in lagoons somewhere, the population could have been reduced to remnant size in a relatively short time. But this is all speculation, and we will probably never know the true reason for the disappearance of this population.

Life History

The gray whale is, like most mysticetes, a strongly seasonal breeder, mating and calving in winter. There is good evidence that this species has a gestation period that is longer than that of most other baleen whales, perhaps 13 months in total. Dr Dale Rice has suggested that the fetus does not grow during the final month of pregnancy. If this is so, it may be an adaptation to the gray's long migration. Remaining within the womb would facilitate efficient nutrient transfer between mother and offspring, and would also mean that the mother is not burdened with an independent calf while migrating. Such a state would also diminish the calf's vulnerability to any predation en route.

Calves are about 15 ft (4.6 m) at birth, and, at least in the eastern Pacific, most enter the world within the confines of shallow coastal lagoons, where they nurse for some weeks before beginning the long migration north. Calves are weaned by about seven months of age. Sexual maturity is reached between 5 and 11 years, and most females give birth to a single calf every two years.

Little is known about the life expectancy of gray whales, but if it is similar to that of other baleen whales they are probably long-lived. Killer whales are known to attack and even kill gray whales on occasion. During an experiment conducted by scientists off California, migrating grays responded to playbacks of killer whale vocalizations by hiding in inshore beds of giant kelp. The frequency with which such mortalities occur is unknown, but the hiding behavior suggests that predation represents a significant threat at certain times in this whale's life.

Diet

Gray whales are the only large whales that feed primarily on the seafloor, suctioning benthic organisms such as amphipods from the mud. To do this, they roll onto one side to plough the seafloor, and the huge tongue acts much like a piston in this vacuuming process. Interestingly, most gray whales show a preference for a right-side-down roll in this behavior, as evidenced by much greater wear on the baleen on that side of the mouth. This tendency to lateralization in certain behaviors, similar to our handedness, has also been observed in humpback, fin and blue whales.

Gray whales are not exclusively benthic feeders; on occasion, they also feed on small fish in mid water, and sometimes are even observed lunging at the surface. Although they do not eat in winter, grays clearly begin to feed on the northward migration.

Social Organization and Behavior

Virtually everything we know about the social behavior of gray whales comes from studies conducted on the eastern North Pacific population. During summer, they are found alone or in small groups and, as with all mysticetes, group stability over time is not evident. Since the capture of benthic invertebrates is not facilitated by cooperative feeding (as is the case, for example, with humpbacks feeding on small schooling fish), there is no reason to expect coordinated foraging by gray whales.

A gray whale calf rests on its mother's back. Although many features of the gray whale suggest that it is a primitive species, it appears to have evolved in the comparatively recent geological past. The gray whale's taxonomic status is the subject of debate, with some researchers believing that it is related to the rorquals.

As southbound gray whales come closer to the breeding areas of Baja California, social activity increases. Recent studies using night-vision scopes have shown that gray whales migrate faster during the hours of darkness, perhaps reflecting fewer social interactions at this time. On the breeding grounds themselves, pregnant females and new mothers cluster inside the lagoons, while other whales largely remain outside. Sexual activity is frequently seen, sometimes with more than one male actively courting a female. It has been suggested from whaling data that most conceptions occur early in the winter (in late November or early December), with a minority of females mating in January.

Catch History and Conservation Status

Charles Scammon, in his book *The Marine Mammals of the Northwestern Coast of North America* (1874), said: 'None of the species are so constantly and variously pursued as the one we have endeavoured to describe; and the large bays and lagoons, where these animals once congregated, brought forth and nurtured their young, are already nearly deserted… ere long it may be questioned whether this mammal will not be numbered among the extinct species of the Pacific'.

The gray whale's habits certainly rendered it more vulnerable to rapid eradication than any other whale. Highly coastal in its distribution, with a heavy reliance upon lagoons for calving, it also has a tendency to swim in shallow waters very close to shore, making escape from pursuit difficult. The latter characteristic is particularly true of mothers and calves, which were always the most vulnerable animals in a population. Not surprisingly, therefore, whalers found the gray whale an easy prey, although its reputation for violence when pursued gave more than a few harpooners pause.

Intensive whaling for gray whales began along the coast of California in the 19th century. The species was hunted in large numbers from ships, and from a multitude of shore stations which sprang up along the coast. The discovery of the calving lagoons in Baja California precipitated a great slaughter, and the population was rapidly depleted. The last old-style shore station dedicated to this species closed shortly after 1900, and at this time many considered the whale to be extremely rare. However, modern whalers continued to take gray whales in the North Pacific until the species was completely protected in 1947, by which time the population had been drastically reduced.

Western gray whales fared no better. Hunted by Japanese coastal whalers for centuries, they were also taken in large numbers by American and other pelagic operations in the Sea of Okhotsk, Sea of Japan and off Korea. Whaling continued well into the 20th century, and in fact Korea was still hunting western grays until the 1960s. This exploitation so depleted the population that as late as 1974 a scientific paper was published announcing (fortunately mistakenly) that the western gray whale was extinct. Soviet scientists rediscovered the remnant population shortly afterwards.

Today, the eastern population has made a full recovery, and indeed has been one of the great success stories of conservation. Recent estimates have put the population size at around 21,000 animals, and eastern gray whales were recently removed from the endangered species list. Eastern gray whales are still hunted in small numbers by the native people of the Chukotka Peninsula in arctic Russia, but this catch has little impact upon what is clearly a thriving population.

The situation is quite different for the western stock, whose dismal state is often overlooked in all the celebration over the California gray's recovery. There has been little research on the western population, which is clearly among the world's most critically endangered large whales. Estimates put the size of this stock at 250 animals, but too little is known of its true status, and research in this area is urgently required.

The largest known threat to the population is intensive offshore oil and gas development planned for waters off the northeastern coast of Sakhalin Island in the Okhotsk Sea; the site is in the middle of prime feeding habitat for the western gray whale. Other threats may well exist. In particular, it is disturbing that we do not know where this animal breeds. If, like the California gray whale, it relies upon coastal lagoons for calving, it may be extremely vulnerable to exploitation or to coastal development and other human-related threats.

*Like swimming rocks, gray whales carry a large load of barnacles, seen here all over this animal's head and body.
Since (unlike the cyamids colonizing right whale callosities) they do not feed off the whale, the barnacles are not true parasites;
rather, they use the whale as a base from which to filter plankton from the surrounding water.*

Sperm Whale

Of all divers, thou hast dived the deepest. That head, on which the upper sun now gleams, has moved amid the world's foundations. Where unrecorded names and navies rust, and untold hopes and anchors rot, where in her murderous hold this frigate earth is ballasted with bones of millions of the drowned, there in that awful water-land, there was thy most familiar home.

Herman Melville: *Moby Dick*

Scientific name: *Physeter macrocephalus* ('blower' + 'long head'. There remains considerable contention about whether the sperm whale should be called *P. macrocephalus* or *P. catodon*, and some scientists use the latter).

Other common names: cachalot (occasionally used in English, but more commonly in other languages).

Maximum length: males 62 ft (19 m), females 42 ft (13 m).

Distribution: deep water in all oceans. Mature males wander as far as polar waters, while females and juveniles remain in tropical or subtropical latitudes for much of the year.

General Characteristics

Before I had ever seen a sperm whale, a colleague told me that this species 'looked like nothing else on Earth'. When I finally saw one, I realized that he was right. Greatest of all the toothed whales and probably the most ancient of all living cetaceans, the sperm whale is a bizarre animal indeed. With its huge square head, wrinkled skin and small, underslung lower jaw, it is unlike any other animal.

It is unclear how large sperm whales can grow to be. Whalers' stories of 90-ft (27-m) males are obviously exaggerations, and today it is rare to find a member of this species over 52 ft (16 m). But whaling — which often concentrated on the much larger males, notably those found in high latitudes — undoubtedly removed most of the biggest animals from the population. Did 70-ft (21-m) males ever roam the oceans? Since sperm whales are slow to mature and therefore probably very

long-lived, we may have to wait a long time to learn the answer.

The vast head of a sperm whale represents anywhere from 25% to 35% of the animal's total length; the larger proportion is typical of males. The head contains a reservoir of high-quality oil whose appearance gives the whale its common name, since medieval naturalists thought that it was indeed sperm (the oil is called 'spermaceti', which translates to 'sperm of the whale'). The function of this strange fluid is the subject of much debate. The two principal suggestions are that it is used either as a means of regulating buoyancy during the sperm whale's extraordinarily deep dives, or as an acoustic lens to focus sound during echolocation.

At sea, it is difficult to confuse the sperm whale with any other large cetacean. Even the blow is distinctive, since it projects at a forward angle and somewhat to the left. In fact, the sperm whale's single blowhole is located at the front of its head and, with the bizarre asymmetry that one might expect from such an odd animal, is located not on the midline, but somewhat to the left of center. Because of the need to recover from long dives, sperm whales often blow 30 or 40 times before returning to the depths, a marked contrast to the five or six breaths taken by the average baleen whale.

The dorsal fin is small and triangular; that of adult females can be distinguished by the presence of calluses, which are not found on males or immature animals. Aft of the dorsal fin, the tail stock is prominently ridged. The tail is broadly triangular with a deep central notch, and is usually raised at the beginning of a dive. The pattern of scalloping found on the trailing edge of the flukes, together with scars, is used by scientists to identify individuals of this species.

The sperm whale's bizarre nature, which is as obvious in its internal anatomy as in its outward appearance, reflects the great ancientry of its lineage. The species has apparently been a feature of the world's oceans for perhaps as long as 30 million years, far longer than most modern cetaceans.

This remarkable animal was of course immortalized by Herman Melville in *Moby Dick*, the story of Captain Ahab's obsession with finding the huge white sperm whale that had cost him a leg in a previous encounter. Melville himself crewed upon a whaler for a while, and so knew both the industry and its prey very well. His epic tale was supposedly inspired by the true story of an albino sperm whale that various whaling ships had sighted but never managed to kill. Albinos certainly exist in the whale world just as in the human, and there are records of albino humpbacks and right whales from recent times.

Distribution and Movements

Sperm whales can stake a fair claim to being the most oceanic of the great whales. They inhabit all oceans, and rarely enter shallow water. Although they can be found close to the coast in areas where the continental shelf is narrow, or where deep underwater canyons abut the land, their habitat is the great abyssal depths.

Distribution and movements vary considerably by sex and by age. Mature males live primarily in high latitudes, from about 40° to the ice edge, returning to tropical waters only to breed. By contrast, females and their young live in stable groups which generally remain within warm water. Both sexes roam widely in search of food.

Life History

Sperm whale calves are between about 11 and 14 ft (3.5 and 4.5 m) at birth, and are born after a gestation period which, at about 16–17 months, is much longer than that of any baleen whale. This may be related to prolonged development of neural tissue in this large-brained animal. Alternatively, it may be that, unlike mysticetes, sperm whales do not have to telescope pregnancy into a 12-month period to coincide with migratory schedules. Quite when weaning occurs is somewhat a matter of definition. Young sperm whales may well feed on solid food within their first two years, but nursing has apparently been documented in animals as old as 12 years. This strangely protracted maternal care probably serves largely as a reinforcement of mother-offspring bonding rather than as sustenance.

Sexual maturity is reached between about 8 and 12 years in females, and at greater than 10 years in males. Females produce a calf about every five years, although there is good evidence that their reproductive rate declines with age. Older females may invest more effort in the rearing of existing young than in producing new calves. Although males are capable of reproducing while in their teens, it is now thought very unlikely that they do so (see below). Like most large-brained mammals, sperm whales are long-lived: life expectancies exceeding 60 years for both sexes are quite likely.

Diet

Although sperm whales do not live exclusively off deep-water prey, much of the animal's foraging is done at extraordinary depth. Easily the most accomplished diver of any mammal, the sperm whale spends much of its life in a remote and lightless world far below the surface. One sperm whale was found entangled in ocean-floor telephone cable at 3700 ft (1130 m), while, even more remarkably, another was tracked to a depth of 9200 ft (2800 m), or almost two miles below the surface.

Yet another extraordinary indication of this animal's diving ability is the record of a sperm whale killed by a whaling vessel off Durban, South Africa, in 1969 after a dive which had lasted almost two hours. In this whale's stomach were two recently ingested sharks of a species (*Scymnodon*) that is known to live on the sea floor. Since the depth in the area was almost 10,000 ft (3050 m), it is assumed that the sperm whale descended that far to forage. The pressure at such a depth is enormous – more than 300 atmospheres – yet sperm whales appear to be limited in their diving by time (and oxygen) rather than pressure. How do they accomplish this remarkable feat?

A sperm whale in calm waters takes one of many breaths to repay its oxygen debt after a long dive. The spout of this species is unusual in that it projects forward and slightly to the left of the head, reflecting the oddly asymmetrical placement of the sperm whale's single blowhole.

'This whale, among the English of old vaguely known as the Trumpa whale, and the Physeter whale, and the Anvil Headed whale, is… without doubt, the most formidable of all whales to encounter; the most majestic in aspect; and lastly, by far the most valuable in commerce.' Herman Melville: *Moby Dick*

As far as most of the animal is concerned, the pressure is not quite the problem that it may seem. Whales, like us, are composed primarily of water, and water is essentially incompressible. The real problem for a deep diving animal is the difference between the pressure of its body cavities (notably the lungs) and that of the water outside. Sperm whales get around this neatly by collapsing their lungs as they dive. However, the finer points of their diving physiology are not well understood. Certainly, it is difficult for us humans, limited as we are to the surface realm, to understand how an air-breathing mammal can survive, let alone function, under such extraordinary conditions.

Squid, including the giant squid, Architeuthis, is the principal prey, but sperm whales also eat octopus and various kinds of fish, including bottom-dwelling species such as the deep-water sharks mentioned previously. How a sperm whale locates its food is no mystery. Its echolocation system is highly advanced, and the animal can, perhaps quite literally, 'see' in sound; thus the darkness of the great ocean depths is no impediment to its foraging. But how does it subdue and catch squid and other food? The intuitive belief that the prey is always gripped and crushed using the mouth is confounded by whaling records of healthy sperm whales with broken lower jaws; in one case, a large male with a stomach full of squid was found to be completely missing its lower jaw! Many years ago, Dr Ken Norris proposed a still controversial theory that sperm whales can echolocate actively, that is, use concentrated bursts of sound as a weapon to stun or kill prey. While this idea is far from accepted, it would explain how sperm whales could subdue even giant squid, maximizing their use of time and energy in the extraordinarily high-pressure environment in which they forage.

Like many other – perhaps all – toothed whales, it is probable that sperm whales are suction feeders. Anyone who tried to take a floating object into their mouth in a bath or swimming pool can appreciate the problem facing an aquatic organism: water pressure always pushes the object away. The anatomy of many whales seems to be adapted for suction feeding, with the tongue acting somewhat like a piston; sperm whales are probably no different in this regard.

Social Organization and Behavior

Sperm whales possess a highly evolved social system which stands in sharp contrast to that of baleen whales. Work by Dr Hal Whitehead and colleagues has shown that females live in tightly knit groups, and genetic analysis has recently confirmed that these consist of related animals. These family units appear to share maternal duties: when the older animals are diving deeply to forage, they do so on a staggered schedule so that calves, which remain close to the surface, are never unaccompanied. Groups remain within acoustic contact during foraging dives, with each whale emitting an individually distinctive 'signature' call, or coda.

Males leave these groups at about the age of six years, and migrate to high latitudes. Sometimes alone, and sometimes in small 'bachelor' groups, they feed in polar waters, fueling their growth until such time as they can actively compete with large males for females. It is likely that males do not breed until their twenties, not only because they cannot compete with physically mature older males, but also because females may reject young whales as potential mates. Fully mature males migrate back to tropical waters during the breeding season. Males roam between female groups during this time, and it is possible that aggressive interactions occur between suitors.

Despite their size, there is ample evidence that sperm whales are threatened by predation from killer whales. They respond to such threats by grouping together in a circular formation known from its shape as a marguerite. It is not clear how often predators succeed in killing calves or other members of a sperm whale group, but this cooperative defense is yet another example of the high level of social organization in this species.

Catch History and Conservation Status

The high-quality oil that resides inside the head of a sperm whale proved to be the animal's undoing. Spermaceti is a pure oil that burns cleanly in lamps or candles, and lubricates at extremes of temperature better than any petroleum product. Indeed, a lubricant of equivalent quality has only recently been synthesized from the jojoba plant. It was this extraordinary oil that created a huge industry, that sent men away from their homes on voyages of several years, and that brought many a whaling captain sufficient wealth to support a long and prosperous retirement.

As described elsewhere in this book, sperm whaling seems to have begun off the American island of Nantucket around 1712. By 1780, more than a hundred whalers were engaged in the sperm whale fishery in both the North and South Atlantic. In 1789, the English ship *Amelia* became the first whaler to round Cape Horn and enter the Pacific; she returned a year later carrying 139 tons of sperm whale oil, a huge prize which sent many others off to follow her track. Other whaling grounds were soon discovered, many of them by whalers from the island that had started it all. Of all ports involved in the business of whaling, Nantucket was the greatest for many years. Its ships routinely traveled to the other side of the world in search of sperm whales.

In 1859, the discovery of petroleum in the United States created a new and cheaper source of lighting than sperm oil, and whaling voyages became fewer and less profitable. However, the fishery had started to decline prior to this, probably because overhunting had decimated sperm whale populations in most traditional whaling grounds. With the opening of the Antarctic grounds in 1904, whalers found new populations of sperm whales to exploit, and new markets in which to sell the products.

Some 400,000 sperm whales were slaughtered in the southern hemisphere this century. Much of the whaling for this species was concentrated in high latitudes, taking a preponderence of large males in the mistaken belief that these could be easily replaced in the reproductive pool by younger animals. We now have good evidence that this is not the case, and that females will not simply accept younger males as mates because of a shortage of older suitors. In addition, the whaling policy had a rather more straightforward impact: there are now far fewer males to roam the tropics during the breeding season, and the resulting lower frequency of male-female encounters may well have caused the birth rate to decline.

Today, although this highly oceanic species is among the most difficult of all whales to count and study, it is generally assumed that sperm whales remain fairly abundant in the world's oceans. However, in light of the time lag required for younger males to attain breeding status, and the slow reproductive rate of the species in general, we do not know how long it will take for populations to recover from the excesses of whaling.

'Neptune's treasure'

No chapter can be written on sperm whales without mention of ambergris, also known as 'Neptune's treasure'. Ambergris is a hard, waxy substance which appears to be a digestive biproduct. Its property of perfectly fixing fragrances made it highly prized by the perfume industry. C.P. Idyll, in a scientific paper on ambergris, noted with appropriate humor: 'There is something ludicrous and yet pathetic in the contemplation of a fond mother storing a chunk of decaying malodorous flotsam from the seashore in her refrigerator in the vain hope that it will be the means of paying for her son's education. The hope that inspired her action, and which prompts scores of people every day to pick up and treasure the most repulsive pieces of dead flesh, jellyfish, yellowed wax, rubber, and hundreds of other objects tossed on the beaches by the tides, is the expectation that they have found a piece of that romantic and improbable treasure from the sperm whale's intestine, ambergris'.

The real thing possessed tremendous monetary value. In the 19th century, a 53-lb (24-kg) piece of ambergris sold in London for $42,750, and there are records from whaling of chunks weighing several hundred pounds. Sperm whales do sometimes pass ambergris, so there is always a chance that a chunk will wash up on a shoreline somewhere. But, while there are true stories of common folk making their fortunes from such finds, these events were exceedingly rare. Because sperm whales are no longer legally hunted, and trade in sperm whale products is banned, ambergris is now rarely used, but it remains very valuable.

A group of sperm whales gathers at the surface before dispersing on a foraging dive. The blunt, square head contains a huge reservoir of oil whose function is still not clear. Once widely used to light lamps, make smokeless candles and lubricate machinery, the high-grade oil was the greatest prize of 19th-century whalers, who roamed the oceans of the world searching for sperm whales.

Killer Whale

Scientific name:	*Orcinus orca* (there are various translations of this. Both names may be derivatives of the same Latin word, which may mean 'whale', 'killer whale' or even 'tuna', on which orcas are known to feed. There is currently debate about whether killer whales comprise more than a single species).
Other common names:	orca.
Maximum length:	males close to 33 ft (10 m), females 28 ft (8.5 m)
Distribution:	all oceans, tropics to poles.

General Characteristics

Without a doubt, the killer whale is the most supreme predator in the oceans. The highly developed social structure of this species lends itself to pack hunting; this, together with their size and speed, makes them a potential threat to even the largest baleen whales. While not all killer whales feed on mammals, the species is the only cetacean known to regularly eat warm-blooded prey (although there is some thought that the false killer whale, *Pseudorca crassidens*, may also be in this category).

Whether the legendary voracity of this species actually gave it its common name is a matter of dispute. Some say that 'killer whale' derives from a translator's erroneous reversal of the Basque term for this animal, which was supposedly 'whale killer' (so named because it had been observed to attack even large whales). One might also argue the appropriateness of the name, since all cetaceans are carnivores (even the lowly copepod, primary food of the right whale, is an animal!). As usual, Herman Melville put it best, when he said in *Moby Dick*: 'Exception might be taken to the name bestowed upon this whale, on the grounds of its indistinctness. For we are all killers, on land and on sea; Bonapartes and sharks included'.

Whatever the case, killer whales are striking in appearance. Both sexes have a tall dorsal fin, but in mature males this feature is truly extraordinary, reaching a height of almost 6 ft (2 m). The dorsal fin of females and juvenile males is lower and rather more falcate. Males are considerably larger than females, and can reach weights of close to 10 tons. Although the body color is black above, there is a striking white oval patch behind the eye, and the white ventral coloration extends up the animal's flank in the area above the genital slit. There is a gray saddle pattern behind the dorsal fin; scientists use variations in this feature, together with dorsal fin shape and scars, to identify individual orcas.

Distribution and Movements

Killer whales are truly cosmopolitan, and are found everywhere from the tropics to the poles in all oceans of the world. Most populations appear to possess extensive ranges, and one-way movements of almost 1900 miles (3058 km) have been recorded for identified individuals. However, killer whales will often remain in small areas for long periods when prey is abundant, and in some locations animals are seen virtually year-round.

There is no good evidence for large-scale seasonal migrations in this species. Killer whales inhabiting widely different regions, such as polar and tropical waters, probably represent separate populations rather than a single migratory stock. The movements of all populations are probably related largely to shifts in local abundance of prey.

Two distinct forms of the killer whale were recognized by scientists in the Pacific Northwest as early as the 1970s and probably represent different species. Termed 'residents' and 'transients' at the time because of perceived differences in movement patterns, these names have stuck, although subsequent research has shown that the terms are not strictly appropriate. As described below, residents and transients have major differences in movements, prey, behavior, social structure and overall ecology. Killer whales studied elsewhere in the world also appear to conform to this division. Recently, a possible third type, named 'offshore', was discovered in waters far from the coast off British Columbia. While these animals seem to resemble the resident type, little is currently known about them.

Life History and Diet

The gestation period of the killer whale is known from studies of captive animals to be about 17 months. Length at birth is between 6.5 and 8 ft (2 and 2.5 m), although this may vary among populations. Calves probably begin to feed on solid food at between one and a half and two years, although nursing may continue for some years after this.

Both males and females reach sexual maturity between about 10 and 17 years. Mature females reproduce at intervals ranging from 2 to 14 years (the average seems to be five), and continue to produce young until the age of about 40, although a few animals seem to be able to reproduce into their late fifties. Both sexes are long-lived, females much more so than males: maximum longevity has been estimated at 50–60 years for males, and 80–90 years or more for females.

Diet varies by type. Broadly speaking, resident orcas feed on fish, while transients prey on marine mammals. Overall, a vast array of prey has been recorded, including many types of fish, squid, seabirds, otters, dolphins and porpoises, sirenians (manatees and dugongs) and even some terrestrial mammals. The latter include moose and caribou, which are caught by transients while attempting to cross rivers.

Transients have been observed to attack and sometimes kill large whales. Small minke whales are probably taken quite frequently in some areas, but killer whales have been documented to take on even blue whales. The profusion of rake marks on the tails of humpbacks and some other mysticetes suggests that attacks by killer whales are common. The evidence indicates that most such events represent 'testing' of the prey and do not result in a kill, but young baleen whale calves on migration may be particularly vulnerable to orca attack.

As one would expect from animals feeding on such different prey as fish and mammals, the foraging techniques of residents and transients are quite specialized. Both types employ pack-hunting techniques much of the time, cooperating in order to maximize detection and capture of prey. In residents, this can mean herding a fish school into a tighter ball to facilitate feeding. Faced with more intelligent prey, transients have developed some fascinating strategies. The most spectacular is practiced by the killer whales of Argentina and the Crozet Islands. There, orcas will rush up a beach with a wave to snatch a sealion or elephant seal pup before sliding back into the water. In other areas, transients seem to have solved a problem presented by seals hiding underwater in caves by breathing on a staggered schedule. This ensures that some whales will always be submerged and thus in a position to see and catch the seal when it finally has to leave its hiding place and come up for air. Transient orcas are also quieter than residents, and often become completely silent when foraging in order to not advertize their approach to wary seals or cetaceans.

Another indication of the intelligence and social development of killer whales is their frequent sharing of prey among group members. In addition, there is good evidence that older orcas teach prey-hunting techniques to younger members of a pod.

There is a remarkable true story concerning a cooperative fishery between humans and orcas which occurred in the last century at Twofold Bay in Australia. For many years, a pod of orcas worked together with the whalers from this small New South Wales town, alerting them to the presence of passing right whales by lobtailing in the harbor, then herding the hapless animals towards the whalers' boats. When a whale was killed, the orcas would be given the tongue as payment for their services.

Social Organization and Behavior

Thanks to some outstanding long-term studies pioneered by the late Dr Mike Bigg and his colleagues, we probably know more about the social structure of killer whales than that of any other cetacean. Killer whale societies – at least among residents – seem to be organized in a hierarchical manner. The basic social unit is called an 'intra-pod'.

Three killer whales engage in a behavior called spyhopping, in which they raise their heads far out of the water, apparently in an attempt to look around above the surface. The striking black and white markings of this species, including the eye patch, are clearly displayed here. Note also the huge paddle-shaped flippers.

This is a matrilineal group made up of between two and nine animals who are closely related (i.e. an older female and her direct descendants). Intra-pods include whales of both sexes and may include up to four generations. The members of an intra-pod are always together. A 'subpod' consists of from one to about a dozen intra-pods which associate with each other about 95% of the time; they probably represent a second order of relatedness.

The next level of organization, the 'pod', contains one to three sub-pods. On average, there are about a dozen whales in a pod, although pods containing almost 60 animals have been observed. The groups within a pod associate together about half the time, and probably contain whales which, while more distantly related to one another than those within sub-pods or intra-pods, nonetheless share a common maternal descent. As pods grow, splits into separate pod groupings occur, but generally only over the course of many years.

Killer whales are highly vocal animals, and research on their communication has revealed some fascinating things. Each pod appears to have a particular 'dialect', comprising sounds that are unique to the animals within it, as well as other sounds that are shared by other pods. Remarkably, the degree of similarity in dialects among different pods seems to be directly correlated with the degree of relatedness between them. In other words, the dialects reflect common ancestry, or lack of it.

Dispersal, in which the members of one or both sexes (in mammals, it is generally males), leave their natal group, is unknown among resident killer whales. Evidently, residents stay with their families for life. There is limited dispersal among transients: females seem to leave their natal group at maturity or with the birth of their first calf, effectively forming their own pod. Research conducted by Dr Robin Baird has suggested that all sons except the firstborn leave a transient group on reaching sexual maturity. Transient pods are generally smaller than those of resident killer whales, probably to maximize foraging efficiency on the former's mammalian prey.

In addition to the obvious differences in ecology between residents and transients, compelling support for the idea that the two types are undergoing speciation comes from the fact that they never associate with one another, even when traveling in the same area. Indeed, they often appear to actively avoid one another. Whether the mammal-eating transients ever attempt to kill calves or other members of resident pods is unknown, but occasional observations of residents attacking transients may reflect a sort of pro-active defense strategy.

Remarkably, mating has never been observed in killer whales. It is assumed that resident groups outbreed, that is, males either temporarily leave their natal pod to seek mates in another group, or that mating occurs when different pods meet.

Catch History and Conservation Status

Killer whales have never been the subject of an extensive human fishery. Sporadic hunting of this species has occurred at various times, notably in the Antarctic and North Atlantic. In addition, there are isolated native fisheries which occasionally take orcas; examples include the Caribbean island of St. Vincent and the Indonesian island of Lembata.

Humans have sometimes regarded killer whales as competitors for fish, and have occasionally instituted culls. One of the more dramatic examples was the slaughter of large numbers of killer whales by the Icelandic navy in the 1960s. In addition, the aquarium industry has decimated some populations in its rush to display captive killer whales, whose huge public appeal has made them big money-makers. A total of 67 animals was captured from the Pacific Northwest in just five years in the 1960s. In light of what we now know of killer whale society, this act must have wreaked havoc on the social integrity of the pods concerned.

Overall, orcas are abundant and do not represent a major conservation concern. However, the levels of pollutants that they carry are among the highest in any cetacean, and we do not yet know whether these contaminants represent a serious threat to the wellbeing of this remarkable animal.

An adult killer whale breaches in the waters of the Pacific Northwest. Here, three decades of long-term studies based upon identified individuals have taught us much about the biology and behavior of this beautiful and highly social animal. Among the most widely distributed of all the cetaceans, orcas are found from the tropics to the poles in both hemispheres.

Whaling: The Taming of Leviathan

*He visited this country also with a view to catching horse-whales, which had
bones of very great value for their teeth, of which he brought some to the king. The best whales were catched in his own
country, of which some were forty-eight, some fifty yards long.*

King Alfred's account of Ottar's voyage, AD 890

Earliest Days

The hunting of whales by mankind has a long history. The origins of whaling are lost in the distant past, and we do not know precisely when humans first took the remarkably courageous step of setting out to pursue and kill one of the great whales. The motive for such a hunt is not hard to guess: it is very likely that, whoever these first whalers were, they came from a community which had previously benefitted from stranded whales. A huge carcass washed up on the shore must have represented a vast bounty of meat, oil and other products for poor coastal people, and it cannot have been too long before local fishermen began to entertain the idea of actively pursuing one of the huge creatures that they occasionally saw from their boats. There must have been much talk, and much trepidation, before someone finally dared to attempt this astonishing feat. We can only imagine the fear that they must have felt at dealing with such a vast and powerful animal from so frail and vulnerable a platform as a small open boat.

But eventually someone, somewhere, succeeded in killing a whale; and in so doing, they effected a small but critical change in mankind's view of these monsters of the sea. No longer was the whale an unattainable mystery of the deep, but rather something which, as terrifying as it might still be, could now be subdued and turned to human needs. Thus began the long march towards modern commercial whaling and the routine, mechanized slaughter which in our time has threatened the very existence of some species of whales.

A number of quite ancient cultures whaled at least sporadically. We know that the Persians occasionally hunted whales some four thousand years ago, and archaeological evidence suggests that whaling was an important activity for the Phoenicians in the Mediterranean. The Japanese have a long tradition of coastal whaling, going back to at least the 16th century when a method was devised for driving whales into large nets. In the Arctic, there is no doubt that sea mammals of various kinds were routinely taken long ago by Inuit (Eskimo) peoples, and these animals remain a fundamental part of Inuit life and culture in many areas today.

A particularly wasteful fishery was practiced by prehistoric natives in various places along the northern rim of the Pacific. Whales would be shot with darts tipped with the lethal poison aconite. Since it would take some time for the animal to die, the whalers were presumably dependent upon a portion of their 'catch' remaining within the area, and then drifting to shore after death. In most places, this probably happened in a minority (perhaps a small minority) of cases, so that many whales were killed and not utilized. Gray whales are known to have been the target of this fishery, and perhaps right whales were too.

With the exception of the Phoenicians, it is probable that most of these historical hunts were of the subsistence type, undertaken primarily for the purpose of supplementing a diet that came from fishing or coastal agriculture. In many areas, whale meat or other products would certainly have been traded with communities inland, but not for profit in the commercial sense. A parallel can be found today in the traditional whaling which occurs from the village of Lamalera on the Indonesian island of Lembata. Men from Lamalera regularly kill sperm whales and other cetaceans in local waters. After the flesh has been dried, village women set out on a day-long walk into mountain communities where the meat is exchanged for vegetables and root crops.

The Beginning of the Chase: The Great Basque Fishery

The advent of true commercial whaling, in which whales were killed and sold for money rather than local needs, probably began in Europe in early medieval times. There are dim echoes of what may have been a commercial hunt prior to this. In the year 890, an adventurer named Ottar returned to Saxon England from a voyage of discovery to the White Sea and reported to King Alfred that Norwegians killed huge whales – probably right whales. However, we do not know whether this activity fulfilled the definition of a commercial hunt in terms of being conducted with some regularity, and solely for profit. The people who are generally credited with initiating such an enterprise are the Basques of southern France and northern Spain. Medieval market records tell us that the Basques were regularly taking whales in the Bay of Biscay as early as the 11th century.

First, however, it is worth considering the early whalers' choice of prey. For various reasons, not all whales were equally available to them. Some, such as blue and fin whales, were simply too fast to be caught by men whose only source of propulsion on the water was wind on a sail, or the strength of their own arms applied to oars. Indeed, most of the rorquals remained largely immune from human exploitation for centuries. Some whales, such as the bowhead, lived in the inaccessible and unknown Arctic or, like the sperm whale, were rarely to be found in the shallow coastal waters to which whaling was inevitably confined during its early years. Others, such as humpbacks, while slow and often coastal in their habitats, frequently sank when killed, making active recovery impossible in most circumstances. Instead, whalers would have to hope that they could retrieve the animal some days later when decomposition had set in and gases inside the whale buoyed the carcass to the surface. More often than not, wind or currents would take the animal's body far from land and it would be lost.

While solutions to some of these problems were gradually fashioned, one species was unfortunate enough to present none of these difficulties. The northern right whale was a perfect target for early whalers. Slow and easy to pursue, and a frequent inhabitant of coastal waters, the right whale's thick layer of blubber generally caused it to float when killed. Thus whalers could potentially kill a number of these animals and tow the floating carcasses into shore for processing. In addition, the right whale yielded an enormous quantity of meat, as well as oil and baleen of high quality. All of these characteristics probably gave the right whale its name – it was considered simply the 'right' whale to kill.

Quite when right whaling as a sustained commercial enterprise began we do not know. The earliest record dates from 1059, when an administrative decree was issued regarding whale meat in the market at the port of Bayonne in southern France. A later document tells us that the French king, apparently ever eager to seek new sources of revenue, imposed a tax on the tongues of whales landed at Bayonne and Biarritz; it seems that the huge tongue of a right whale was considered a popular gastronomic item at the time.

The early Basque whaling industry, such as it was, seems to have been a collaborative effort between all of the fishermen in a town. Men were paid to keep a full-time watch for whales from towers constructed for this purpose. When a whale was sighted, the alarm was sounded and fishermen would quickly launch small rowing boats and set off in pursuit. We have little idea of how efficient these men were as killers. It is likely that many whales were 'struck and lost' – harpooned but never caught, often to die later from their wounds. We do know that the Basques had a preference for mothers and calves: a calf was easy to kill and, in so doing, the whalers would often be likely also to capture the mother because of the latter's tendency to remain protectively with her offspring. This habit of killing both calves and reproductively mature females undoubtedly accelerated the decline of the right whale population in European waters.

The Basques were to dominate European whaling for many years, and their skills in the craft were so well developed that several centuries later Basque harpooners were still avidly sought for service on the whaling vessels of other countries. In an effort to retain control over this expertise, the Spanish crown forbade the Basques – at one

A dead minke whale is hauled onto the deck of a Norwegian whaling vessel after being harpooned. Modern whaling inherits a tradition that goes back almost a thousand years to the days when Basque fishermen first hunted right whales in the Bay of Biscay. Today, however, the industry has little in common with the whaling practices of medieval times. Modern whales are pursued by fast motorized catcher boats, killed with explosive harpoons, and rapidly processed on floating factory ships or at highly mechanized land stations. The main products derived from whales are meat and oil, although most of the animal is utilized for a variety of products.

The minke in the photo bears silent witness to the long history of overhunting that has characterized modern whaling. Once considered too small to be worth killing, this little whale is now the principal target of Japanese and Norwegian whaling operations. Minkes bear the brunt of current commercial hunts for the simple reason that most of the larger and more valuable species were recklessly overexploited. Although generally considered to be abundant worldwide, the species has certainly not been taken in low numbers: this century, more than 100,000 minkes have been killed in the southern hemisphere alone.

point under penalty of death – to pursue such employment, but many ignored this prohibition and worked elsewhere anyway.

It was almost certainly the Basques who first ventured across the North Atlantic in search of pristine whaling grounds in the New World. There is some evidence that Basques may have 'discovered' the Americas more than a century before Columbus made his infamous voyage, but we cannot be sure. Certainly, they were present in the region by the early 1500s: historical records indicate that the Basques maintained several whaling camps on the Labrador coast in or near the Strait of Belle Isle from at least 1530 on. The most important of these was at a place called Red Bay, where 20 to 30 Basque whalers could regularly be found at anchor in the summer months. Recent archaeological excavations at Red Bay have revealed that the Basques were hunting substantial numbers of both right and bowhead whales. The occurrence of the latter species off southern Labrador is interesting, since no bowheads are found there today. It seems probable that the range of this ice-loving whale was shifted south during this period as a result of a major climatic event known as the 'Little Ice Age'. This brought declining temperatures to formerly mild regions and effectively closed off Greenland and other northern areas with impenetrable pack ice; it was at this time that the famous frost fairs were held on the River Thames in London.

Declines, Explorations and New-Found Grounds

By the beginning of the 17th century we begin to see records noting the scarcity of whales on the known whaling grounds. Shortly after 1600, whalers responded to declining catches by expanding their activities to high-latitude areas of the northeastern Atlantic, including such forbidding areas as eastern Greenland and the islands of Spitsbergen and Jan Mayen. Exploring these remote waters in search of new right whale stocks, the whalers instead discovered substantial populations of that most polar of all whales, the bowhead. William Scoresby, a remarkable English whaling captain who published thorough and careful observations relating to whales in the early 19th century, noted that

bowheads were abundant in the bays around Spitsbergen and Jan Mayen. 'Never having been disturbed,' he wrote, 'these animals were unconscious of danger, and allowed themselves to be so closely approached, that they fell an easy prey to the courageous fishermen'.

Guided by Basque harpooners and crew, Dutch and German whalers, followed by the British, pursued this fishery relentlessly, in spite of often terrible weather and difficult conditions. Spurred by prices for whale oil and baleen so high that a ship could sometimes recoup an entire season's expenses with the capture of a single bowhead, new grounds were opened and fished out: first off western Greenland during the 18th century, then around Baffin Island and areas to the northwest. By the middle of the 19th century the hunt for Atlantic bowheads was effectively over.

By this time, however, elements of the whaling industry had long since begun to venture far afield in search of new whales and new profits. This expansion, which was truly worldwide in nature, was born in the ports of New England in the northeastern United States. New Englanders had probably begun to whale in local waters shortly after the first settlers arrived. When the *Mayflower* Pilgrims ended a particularly miserable voyage across the Atlantic at what is now Provincetown at the tip of Cape Cod, Massachusetts, they were astonished at the number of whales they found there. They wrote that 'We saw a great many whales of the best kind for oil and bone,' (i.e. right whales; the 'bone' being whalebone, or baleen), adding that they wished that they had brought with them implements for whaling. 'Every day,' wrote William Bradford, their leader, 'we saw whales playing hard by us.' Another early settler wrote in his journal that they felt they could almost 'walk across Cape Cod Bay upon the backs of right whales.' Local legend has it that the first shot fired by one of the Pilgrims in the New World was fired from the deck of the *Mayflower* at a passing right whale. Ironically, the shooter almost killed himself, since the gun exploded; but the act was an omen of things to come.

The Pilgrims and their descendants were taught the rudiments of whaling by the local Nauset Indians, who had long used 'drift' (stranded) whales and who occasionally attempted to pre-empt Nature and take a live one. Whaling began in earnest in the second half of the 17th century, and the overexploitation that was a hallmark of the industry everywhere rapidly depleted local populations of right and humpback whales. As Sir Sidney Harmer, an eminent British scientist, noted tersely in 1928, 'The history of their pursuit followed the usual course.' By 1750, there was very little whaling in Massachusetts waters. Nonetheless, the local exploitation had given birth to a formidable industry that was to dominate the world's whaling trade for many years. For almost two hundred years, whalers from New England ports sailed to the ends of the Earth in pursuit of their quarry, opening up many new whaling grounds and sometimes providing the first contact that local people had ever had with Americans.

No port was more adventurous in this exploration, and none more prosperous, than Nantucket. In 1712, a sloop from Nantucket Island was caught by a storm and blown offshore to the edge of the continental shelf, and there discovered abundant sperm whales. For the next century, the island and the whale were to become almost synonymous. Nantucketers set out for voyages that sometimes lasted three or four years, and which eventually opened up new whaling grounds as far away as Japan and the South Seas. While whales of many kinds were taken, the sperm whale, valued for its highly prized oil, was the chief target. The wealth that this animal brought to many captains and vessel owners can still be glimpsed today in the beautiful houses on the island.

Everywhere that whalers, of all nationalities, went the story was the same: overhunting followed by decline. In the middle of the 19th century, at a time when the Atlantic bowhead and right whale fishery were effectively finished, whalers in the North Pacific discovered new populations of both these species. In 1835, an American whaler named the *Ganges* entered what became known as the Northwest Ground in the Gulf of Alaska and described seeing 'millions of whales'. This was of course a huge exaggeration, but we can see in their words large untouched stocks of whales. Right whaling began in that year, and just 14 years later the population was already so depleted that many whalers turned their attention to the newly discovered stock of bowheads in the western Arctic. New discoveries drew large numbers of whaling vessels to an area. A hundred whalers worked off Japan in 1835. Several hundred could be found in the Bering and Beaufort Seas at the height of Arctic bowhead whaling in the 1860s. Similarly, records indicate that as many as three hundred vessels converged on the Okhotsk Sea in the 1840s to plunder the new population of bowheads that had been found there. Elsewhere, other whalers pursued humpbacks and gray whales, either from sailing ships or from numerous shore stations that sprang up along the west coast of North America. These areas proved profitable for a few years or a couple of decades, and then were fished out.

Modern Whaling

Despite the immense damage done to a few species during this period, the status of the majority of the world's whale populations in the middle of the 19th century was probably quite healthy. Certain species had been barely touched by hunting. In particular, the speed of the rorquals presented an immense difficulty to whalers. As late as 1851, Herman Melville wrote that 'There is no means known to catch the fin whale or its fast cousins', echoing the general frustration of the whaling industry that the largest of all prizes, the finback and the blue whale, for the most part lay beyond the reach of sail and oars.

Yet, less than twenty years after Melville had written these words, everything changed. The cause was two major innovations. In 1868, a resourceful Norwegian whaling captain named Svend Føyn invented the bomb lance, an explosive harpoon. Fired from a gun, the harpoon no longer merely penetrated the whale's body, but instead exploded a charge that frequently debilitated or killed the animal. Suddenly whalers had been given the means to despatch a whale quickly, and often without having to place their boats almost on the animal's back, as was the case with traditional hand-thrown harpoons. While the explosive harpoon did not always work well, it represented a huge step forward technologically. Inevitably, its efficiency and design were gradually

*Two humpback whales travel through the frigid waters off the Antarctic continent. Buffered
against the cold by a thick layer of blubber, humpback and other whales spend the austral summer
in these waters, feasting on vast populations of krill.*

WHALING: THE TAMING OF LEVIATHAN

improved over succeeding years until we find its ultimate incarnation in the large cannons mounted on the bows of modern whale catchers.

Shortly after Føyn's invention changed the way in which whales were killed, the steam engine started to come into use in the whaling industry. Now whalers could chase down even the fastest fin whales, and suddenly all of the rorquals found themselves under the gun.

The Final Frontier: Slaughter in the Antarctic

The turn of the century ushered in a new era of highly mechanized whaling, and also brought the discovery of the richest of all the world's whaling grounds, the Antarctic. This forbidding place at the bottom of the world was first explored by a whaling ship in 1904, and there the crew found whales beyond their wildest dreams. Vast untouched populations of humpbacks, blue whales, finbacks, right and sei whales filled the productive waters of the Southern Ocean. Modern whaling had found its great playground, and a slaughter unparalleled in the history of human hunting was about to begin.

Two final innovations set the stage for this carnage. The compressor permitted whalers to pump pressurized air into the bodies of whales that would otherwise sink, making the recovery and processing of the rorquals much easier. Then in 1925 the first factory ship, the *Lancing*, was introduced into the Antarctic. It is difficult to overestimate the importance of this latter development to whaling companies. Previously, they had been forced either to process whales alongside their ships (a long and complicated ordeal superbly described by Melville in *Moby Dick*), or to rely upon land stations. The latter option meant much time lost in transport, and because of spoilage also limited the catcher boats' range of operation. Furthermore, high taxes were often levied upon whalers (notably by the British) for the use of the land. At a stroke, the factory ship dispensed with all these difficulties. A floating factory with its attendant catcher boats could go anywhere, often far from land, and remain at sea for months at a time. The catchers killed whales, then delivered them to the factory ship, which hauled their carcasses up a slipway on the vessel's stern and rapidly processed

them on deck. Men with huge flensing knives would strip the flesh off the whale, aided by powerful steam winches, then the blubber would be boiled or 'rendered' in huge cookers below decks to extract the vast store of valuable oil. An efficient crew could take a 65-ft (20-m), 50-ton adult fin whale and reduce it to nothing in 45 minutes.

Over the next few decades, the number of whales killed in this region was staggering. Almost three-quarters of a million fin whales were slaughtered, and 360,000 blue whales. These two species bore the brunt of southern hemisphere whaling during an intensive period of exploitation in the 1930s. As stocks of these two giants began to dwindle, the whalers turned increasingly to smaller species: more than 200,000 humpbacks, a similar number of sei whales, almost 400,000 sperm whales – and over 100,000 of the small minke whales that were once considered too small to be worth the effort of catching. In all, more than two million whales were killed and processed in the southern hemisphere this century. In terms of both numbers and sheer biomass, this represents by far the greatest mass-slaughter of wildlife in human history.

Faced with declining catches, even the whalers realized that, if they did not attempt some regulation of their activities, they would be whaling themselves out of business. Various attempts to manage the industry culminated in 1948 with the International Convention for the Regulation of Whaling. This treaty, which all the major whaling nations signed, created the International Whaling Commission (IWC) as a forum for management decisions and to sponsor research on whale stocks. Nonetheless, the industry repeatedly failed to listen to the warnings of the IWC's scientists, and frequently gave the benefit of the doubt to profits rather than to the whales. Despite the establishment of quotas and agreements to protect certain severely depleted species, the IWC largely failed in its mandate to sensibly manage whales as a resource.

Just how dismal was this failure became clear only recently. In late 1993, Dr Alexey Yablokov, a senior Russian scientist, revealed that the Soviet Union had illegally caught huge numbers of whales. Beginning in the late 1940s, they had routinely ignored quotas or protected status, and had essentially killed anything that crossed the bows of their catcher vessels. Some scientists had long suspected that this was the case, but no one could have guessed the extent of the deception. In all, the difference between what the USSR reported to the IWC and what they had actually killed was more than 100,000 whales in the southern hemisphere alone! Humpbacks were particularly badly hit: reporting that they had killed just 2700, the Soviets had actually slaughtered more than 48,000. In addition, Soviet whaling fleets killed large numbers of blue and right whales, which were already severely depleted as a result of the 'regular' excesses of previous whaling.

In retrospect, the clues had been there for all to see. In the late 1950s and early '60s, there was already considerable discussion of how depleted the Antarctic whale stocks were, and much talk of restrictions and reduced operations. Paradoxically, it was at this time that the USSR – far from scaling back – began adding new factory ships to its southern hemisphere whaling fleets. The Soviets also succeeded in delaying for many years the introduction of a regulatory scheme for whaling vessels which would have required independent observers to be present on all ships.

The damage done by illegal Soviet operations may have been enormous in some cases. We do not yet know the full extent of Soviet catches in the northern hemisphere; while these were undoubtedly not as extensive as in the Antarctic populations, some may have been as or more significant. In particular, recent work conducted by Dr Robert Brownell and myself suggests that the Soviets killed many of the remaining northern right whales in the eastern North Pacific. Sightings of this species in the region suddenly became rare in the early 1960s, despite increased searching effort; it was as if the population had disappeared overnight. Suspiciously, at about this time, Soviet scientists were reporting numerous sightings of right whales in the area, and it now seems likely that many of these 'sightings' were actually catches. Today, this population is desperately endangered, and the Soviet Union may possess the dubious distinction of having irreversibly damaged its chances of recovery.

Overall, the whaling industry serves as a textbook case of how not to deal with an abundant but limited resource. In particular, its history embodies two common principles of mismanagement which have been 'applied' to everything from rainforest clearance to pollution of air and water. The first is that, in the absence of certainty, the benefit of the doubt is almost always given to the exploiter rather than to the resource. It is all too easy to hide behind inconclusive data, and little of what was known about the size of whale populations could be demonstrated with certainty. The second, related, principle is rather less obvious, but is one which continues to obstruct human efforts to forestall environmental problems at all scales. It is simply that one can never demonstrate that a major problem would have actually occurred, had one not taken preventative measures. Sadly, the corollary to this is that it is quite easy to demonstrate the economic consequences, such as reduced profits or loss of jobs, that frequently accompany such prevention. Thus a corporate entity finds it all too easy to rebuff attempts to proactively head off a disaster by pointing to the human consequences. The whaling industry has frequently exploited both of these principles, and continues to do so today.

It is tempting to rationalize away all of whaling's excesses and mistakes in various ways. In some cases the rationalizations are quite reasonable. After all, medieval whalers saw themselves as existing in an uncertain cosmos pervaded by superstition and ruled by an omnipotent god who controlled everything, including the whales. They could hardly be expected to understand the idea of resource conservation and management. This excuse is much more difficult to extend to the Norwegians who, in a burst of whaling around 1900, probably wiped out the few northern right whales remaining in European waters. And by the time we reach the era of the illegal Soviet catches, we can claim no such innocent view of our interactions with the natural world.

Whaling has been greatly reduced in recent years, but it has far from disappeared. It is too early to state that the world's whales, many of which we once brought perilously close to extinction, are now forever safe from the predations of mankind.

Whale Research

...to pursue our research in the unfathomable waters.
Georges Cuvier

Scientific research on large whales has increased greatly in the last two decades. In particular, long-term studies of identified individuals have taught us much about the biology and behavior of these fascinating animals. Research also has a major role to play in their conservation, since we cannot protect a population unless we know enough about it to formulate wise management strategies.

The largest difficulty that we face in attempting to assess the current status of the world's whale populations stems from a fundamental fact about any large whale: despite their often immense size, these are animals that are often exceedingly difficult to see and to count. Whales are (with the exception of some humans in airline frequent-flier programs!) the widest-ranging of all mammals, traveling thousands of miles between feeding and breeding grounds and often wandering endlessly over large distances in search of food. Worse, they live in an ocean environment that is frequently inhospitable or dangerous to human observers. Anyone who has found themselves far from land in a small boat in rough weather will appreciate the immense difficulties that we face in conducting research on whales. Finally, whales are creatures which spend most of their lives underwater, out of our sight. Before we consider the status of whales today, let's take a moment to look at the ways in which scientists attempt to study these elusive animals.

Until recently, most of what we knew about whales came from examination of animals killed by the whaling industry. Although whales are indeed among the most difficult animals to study, it is worth noting that the sample sizes that we have in our data for the most intensively exploited species are among the largest available for any mammal. For example, the IWC's Southern Hemisphere Database, which accumulated biological information from decades of Antarctic whaling, includes information on a staggering 92,000 pregnant female fin whales! There is no comparable sample for any terrestrial mammal.

Much was learned from whaling about those subjects to which the examination of carcasses traditionally lends itself, notably physiology, anatomy and reproduction. The whaling industry also initiated a program of 'marking' whales in order to track their movements. The method involved firing a uniquely numbered stainless steel cylinder from a shotgun into the body of a live whale. The mark was called a 'Discovery tag', after a British scientific body named the Discovery Committee which began the program. The basic idea was that some of these cylinders would be recovered when marked whales were killed and butchered, anywhere from a few days to several years after the original marking. By looking at the number of the cylinder and checking the scientific records, the whalers would know where and when the animal concerned had been marked, and so would learn something about its movements.

Today, whale researchers use a much more efficient technique to study the movements and behavior of whales. As we have seen, it is possible to photographically identify individual whales of many species by variations in their natural markings (such as the unique pattern found on the underside of a humpback whale's tail). This method has obvious advantages over the Discovery tag, since individual whales can be photographically 'recaptured' over and over without the necessity of killing them. Instead of recording just two points in the whale's life (the marking and the recovery), we can build up a large history of sightings, sometimes over many years. From this history we can obtain detailed information about the whale's movements, migrations, reproduction, social affiliations and behavior. In recent years, numerous researchers have established long-term studies of particular populations of whales, and the results have added greatly to our understanding of the biology and behavior of the species concerned. In some cases, identified individuals have been seen hundreds of times over periods as long as twenty years. In studies of humpback and northern right whales, we have observed particular females produce many calves over the years, and have watched as some of those calves have grown up and given birth to calves of their own.

How Many Whales...?

Theoretically, it is also possible to estimate the size of a whale population from this 'mark and recapture' of individually identified whales. Since determining how many whales exist in a particular population is so fundamental to conservation, it is worth taking a moment to consider how we do this – and to stress the problems that make reliable counts very hard to come by. The principle is simple, and works as follows.

A scientist goes out into the field and photographs as many individual whales as possible. Let's say that in the first year of her study she manages to record 100 different whales in her study area (perhaps they are humpback whales, and she is identifying the individuals by photographing each whale's unique tail pattern). The next year, our researcher goes out again and does the same thing. And again, let's assume she photographs 100 humpbacks. Now, it's very likely that some of the individuals that she photographed in the first year will also be in the second year's sample. Common sense says that if the number of individuals that she finds in both years' photographs forms a large percentage of the total number of whales that she has identified, then the entire population is not likely to be much bigger than her total sample.

For example, let's say that when she puts the 200 photographs from both years together and compares them, she finds that she has only 110 individuals. In other words, 90 of the 100 whales that she saw in the first year were also seen in the second. Such a high resighting rate must mean either that the total population isn't much bigger than her total sample of 110, or that the population is very structured and that other portions of it never come into her study area. If, on the other hand, our researcher finds that, out of the 100 individuals she

photographed in her first year, only five appear in the second year's sample of 100 animals, it is very likely that all the whales she has identified represent only a small portion of a much larger population.

There are a variety of statistical methods which use this simple principle to produce a numerical estimate of the population size. However, all of the methods are based upon certain assumptions. If any of these assumptions is not correct, the reliability of the resulting population estimate will be compromised. The extent to which this will be true depends on how, and to what extent, a particular assumption is violated. For example, a major assumption is that all whales have an equal chance of being photographed. If this is not true, either because some individuals are not easily identifiable, or because some never come into the scientist's study area, then this will have an effect on the population estimate.

None of this is terribly interesting to the general public, but it is critically important to the conservation of whales because much of what we do in whale 'management' is based upon the accuracy of population estimates. Unfortunately, because of the tremendous difficulties of working with whales, and their elusive, wide-ranging habits, virtually all attempts to estimate population size involve assumption violations to some extent. Since we cannot temporarily drain an ocean to find out the true number of whales, in most cases we cannot demonstrate how good (or bad) our population estimates really are. This is less true with small, critically endangered populations, but even here we have to invest a great deal of survey effort to obtain reliable counts. There are other ways of counting whales that do not involve the 'mark-recapture' technique, but all methods have problems of their own which frequently affect the results.

High-Tech Solutions

Scientists today use many other techniques for studying whale biology, and some involve high-tech approaches. Three in particular deserve mention. First, we can attach a radio tag to a whale which transmits a signal to a satellite whenever the whale is at the surface. This allows us to monitor the whale's movements far from shore without ever having to go into the field (actually, since whales don't have necks, attaching one of these satellite tags for a prolonged period remains the biggest challenge in this work). In addition to location, such tags can also provide detailed information on a whale's diving behavior, and on characteristics (such as water temperature) of the physical environment through which it travels.

Using this technique, Dr Bruce Mate and colleagues have tracked North Atlantic right whales for many weeks, 'watching' them as they travel up and down the east coast of the United States, and monitoring the characteristics of the water masses in which they attempt to make a living. Dr Mate has also followed Hawaiian humpback whales as they begin their migration north to Alaska in early spring.

Next, powerful new techniques in molecular biology have made genetic analysis an increasingly important tool for the study of whales and other animals. Samples for this work are usually obtained as skin biopsies, generally by shooting a small dart at the whale. The dart harmlessly takes a small punch of skin before bouncing off into the water, in which it floats for easy retrieval. Back in the laboratory, DNA extracted from the skin tissue can be used to answer questions which often cannot be addressed by other means. DNA studies can tell us about population structure, evolutionary history, paternity of offspring, social relationships and many other aspects of a whale's biology and behavior.

Recently, Dr Per Palsbøll and I have collaborated with scientists from seven countries to apply these exciting new molecular techniques on a large scale. Over the course of two years, we obtained skin samples from more than three thousand humpback whales across the entire North Atlantic Ocean, from the West Indies to arctic Norway. During this study, Dr Palsbøll has used DNA to find what are essentially genetic 'tags' — unique genetic markers that unequivocally identify each individual whale. This method of recognizing individuals is actually somewhat superior to the use of artificial tags or photographs of natural markings, since genetic tags are permanent and do not change with time. Using this technique, together with some lucky resamplings, we have tracked individual humpbacks on their migrations — in one case over some

6000 miles (11,000 km) from a feeding ground off Norway to the West Indies breeding range and back again to the feeding area. We have also followed whales from year to year, and even used the genetic data to calculate a population estimate. An additional benefit to such sampling is that the sex of any biopsied animal can be determined using a simple molecular technique. The sex of a whale was previously difficult or impossible to determine, because there are no easily observable external differences between males and females. The lack of such an important and basic item of information about individuals greatly hampered behavioral studies of whales in the past; thus the molecular sexing technique represents a major breakthrough in our research.

Finally, a tremendously exciting window into the whales' world has recently come from an unlikely source: the U.S. Navy. During the Cold War, the Navy established a vast network of hydrophones (underwater microphones) and other devices in both the North Atlantic and North Pacific to listen for Soviet submarines. Because submarines make noise at very low frequencies, below the range of human hearing, this huge listening network was designed primarily to pick up such sounds. While many cetaceans vocalize at higher frequencies, many of the large baleen whales have very 'deep' voices which can easily be detected by the Navy's system. For many years, this system was top secret and so unavailable to whale researchers; but with the collapse of the USSR and the end of the Cold War, suddenly the Navy was willing to open up aspects of this remarkable system to biologists and oceanographers. The results have been astounding. The system has been used to hear whales literally over entire ocean basins, and sometimes to track individual animals over thousands of miles.

These various techniques promise to tell us much about whale biology and behavior in future years. The research that we conduct on whales is sometimes done out of nothing more than curiosity — the simple desire to discover more about these fascinating and mysterious animals. More frequently, however, it is aimed at understanding enough about whales to, we hope, craft sensible conservation strategies that will protect them, as well as the habitats on which they depend.

Conservation

The moot point is, whether Leviathan can long endure so wide a chase, and so remorseless a havoc;
whether he must not at last be exterminated from the waters, and the last whale, like the last man,
smoke his last pipe, and then himself evaporate in the final puff.
Herman Melville: *Moby Dick*

More than a decade has now passed since the International Whaling Commission took the unprecedented step, in 1986, of passing a moratorium on the commercial hunting of whales. Although the exploitation of whales has continued to some extent under various guises, commercial whaling on the scale that was practiced for most of last century is today a thing of the past. As we have seen in the previous chapter, however, the whaling industry inflicted great damage upon most of the world's whales; indeed, it is likely that the populations of some species were reduced by 95% or more of their original sizes. Some, like the northern right whale, were already in danger of extinction by 1900. Most attained this status from the massive and highly mechanized hunting that occurred last century.

What, then, is the status of the world's great whales today as they emerge from this long nightmare of reckless overexploitation? And, having survived whaling, at least for now, what threats face the animals that remain?

Entanglement and Ship Strikes

Apart from a possible resumption of whaling, there are several issues of concern. Some represent known sources of mortality. Other dangers are more complex and their effect is not clear.

The most significant problems in the former category are entanglement and ship collisions. There is a huge quantity of fishing gear of various types scattered throughout the world's oceans, and much of it represents a major source of mortality for marine life. Gill nets, which are generally set like a wall close to the sea floor and left untended for a day or more, kill innumerable cetaceans each year. Large whales are often powerful enough to wrench the nets from their moorings and carry them away, but if the entanglement is serious it may result in the death of the whale from slow starvation. Probably the most destructive form of fishing gear is the drift net, which can sometimes be many miles in length. As the name implies, these nets drift freely until they are recovered, and the toll on marine creatures is often extraordinary. Seals, dolphins, porpoises, large whales, seabirds, turtles and uncounted numbers of non-target species of fish die each year because of this indiscriminate and hugely wasteful fishing method. Whales can also become entangled in various other types of fishing gear, including lobster pot trap lines and long lines.

One of the saddest sights I have seen in my career as a whale biologist was that of a young male humpback whale that stranded alive on a beach on Cape Cod, Massachusetts, in the autumn of 1982. The whale's tail was terribly entangled in a mass of fishing gear, the weight of which was so heavy that it had cut down more than a foot into the animal's flesh. Thus encumbered, the whale had been unable to feed and had slowly starved, probably over a period of many months; indeed, it was so emaciated that parts of its skeleton could be seen — remarkable for a creature whose body is normally so robustly enclosed in fat and muscle. The young humpback died on the beach, and an autopsy revealed that it had started to digest its own stomach.

Several organizations maintain active disentanglement rescue programs for large whales, among them Memorial University of Newfoundland and the Center for Coastal Studies in Massachusetts. In attempting to free whales from entrapments, scientists from the latter institution employ a clever technique borrowed from whaling. Whalers would often attach barrels to the harpoon line so that they could easily track the whale. In addition, the buoyancy of the barrels would significantly slow down the animal, making it much easier for the whalers to kill it. This technique was called 'kegging', since beer kegs were sometimes used. Today, Center scientists attach large floats to a line that is clipped onto whatever fishing gear is around the whale. Just as in whaling days, this eventually slows or stops the animal, making disentanglement much easier.

Whale deaths from ship collisions are a problem wherever whale concentrations coincide with major shipping lanes. Unfortunately, much of the North Atlantic right whale's remaining range does exactly this, particularly in the species' calving grounds off the southeastern United States. The behavior of this luckless species is no help in this matter: right whales are slow and often spend much time at the surface. Worse, when they are sleeping (or whatever the whale equivalent of this activity is), they can be virtually impossible to awaken. As a result, they are highly vulnerable to collisions with fast-moving ships. In the winter breeding season of 1995/6, six right whales died off Florida and Georgia, some because of ship strikes. For a population which now numbers less than three hundred animals, this is a terrifyingly high mortality rate. Ship strike deaths are in fact the largest single concern for this critically endangered population.

Habitat Degradation and Pollution

Because humans do not permanently colonize the aquatic realm, habitat degradation is not as critical an issue for most large whales as it is for large terrestrial mammals. However, there are areas where human development seriously impinges on whale habitat. Increasing coastal development brings more people, more boats and more noise to disrupt critical behaviors such as feeding, mating or nursing. There is evidence that humpback whale mother/calf pairs are now avoiding certain areas in the Hawaiian Islands because of these problems. In other places, oil and gas development and even unregulated whalewatching also create disturbance, although whether this impacts the reproduc-

tive success of the animals is unknown. In addition, the sheer volume of noise from commercial shipping in the world's oceans has radically altered the marine environment. The effect on whale behavior and communication is unclear; however, it is not unlikely that species such as fin and blue whales, which could once hear each other over hundreds of miles, are now increasingly isolated by the unending and ubiquitous cacophony of engines and propellers.

Human development also brings with it one other major scourge, and that is pollution. Obvious sources such as major oil spills create instant mortalities, primarily among smaller marine mammals. It is not clear whether large whales are at high risk from oil, but certainly killer whales are; many died during the famous *Exxon Valdez* spill in Alaska in 1989.

A potentially more serious issue is contaminants, meaning anything from pesticides to industrial chemicals. The impact of these toxins on animal populations is a very complex subject. It is not sufficient to say that simply because a whale's tissues are found to contain high levels of some industrial pollutant that the whale will have a problem. A good example is PCBs, which have been used for decades (in electrical wiring, for example), and which have been dumped in huge quantities into the ocean, or into rivers which drain into the sea. From studies on lab animals, we know that PCBs can seriously impair both immune system function and reproduction. Furthermore, high levels of PCBs have been found in some cetaceans. However, it is unwise to generalize from rodents in a laboratory to cetaceans: they are very different animals in terms of metabolism, fat storage and many other key variables. Concentrations and effect will also vary by age, by sex and by reproductive condition, yet we know very little about how these variables affect either the accumulation or the impact of toxins in cetaceans.

Given the high levels of PCBs and other contaminants in some cetaceans, we have good reason to be concerned that these chemicals may have some negative effect on the animals. Proving this, however, is very difficult. Generally, we would expect the highest quantities of pollutants to occur in animals eating higher on the food chain, since each 'trophic level' magnifies these concentrations. By eating numerous

A group of northern right whales churns the sunset waters off Nova Scotia. Once abundant throughout the North Atlantic and North Pacific, northern right whales were hunted earlier and more intensively than other species. Today, they are the most critically endangered of all large whales, and the remaining populations cling precariously to survival in both oceans.

A truck takes away a dead North Atlantic right whale for autopsy and eventual disposal of the carcass. Critically endangered throughout their range, northern right whales suffer high mortality from fishing gear entanglements and ship collisions, and each death represents a potential blow to the species' chances of recovery.

zooplankton, small fish will each ingest the plankton's combined pollutant burden; whatever eats a lot of these fish magnifies the concentrations further, and so on up the chain. Because of this, we would predict that baleen whales should have lower concentrations of pollutants than odontocetes like dolphins, and this appears to be the case. There is currently no reason to suspect that pollutants have a significant negative impact on populations of baleen whales. However, the issue of transgenerational accumulation is potentially worrying. Since female mammals transfer a large portion of their pollutant burden to their offspring through milk, each generation theoretically inherits greater loads than the one before it. The long-term effects of such accumulation are unknown, as are the impacts that combinations of different pollutants may have on an animal's system.

Three recent examples of mass mortalities among seals and dolphins have all been linked to a morbillivirus of the distemper group, and there is little doubt that this is what killed the thousands of animals concerned. However, some scientists have questioned whether the infected animals were unable to resist the disease because their immune systems had been compromised by high levels of PCBs and other pollutants. At this point, we can say only that the evidence, while not conclusive, is strongly circumstantial. Further research to understand the effect of contaminants on marine mammals is urgently required.

A final threat is that of red tide. Red tides occur when the local population of a particular species of phytoplankton (generally a dinoflagellate called Alexandrium) suddenly explodes. The dinoflagellates produce a natural toxin which is magnified as it moves up the food chain. In high concentrations it can be deadly to mammals and birds, and even humans have been killed (generally from eating shellfish, which efficiently concentrate the toxins through their filter-feeding). Red tide was apparently the cause of a mass mortality of large whales off Cape Cod in 1987, an event which killed at least 15 humpbacks, including many members of my own study population. While these occurrences are 'natural' in that they do not involve any human agents, their frequency appears to have been increasing in recent years. There is good evidence that the population explosions that cause red tides are somehow related to an increase in fresh water in the system. While hurricanes can occasionally trigger such events, a more disturbing source of fresh water is run-off from coastal development. If this connection is valid, we can expect further problems from red tide in highly developed areas in future.

On The Brink: The Most Endangered Populations

Today, most whales appear to be recovering from the nightmare of overhunting to which they were subjected. However, there are some notable exceptions. Which are the most critically endangered populations of large whales today?

It is clear that northern right whales are on the brink of extinction throughout their range. As we have seen, the last remnant of the eastern North Atlantic population was all but eradicated by Norwegian whaling at the turn of the 20th century. In the eastern North Pacific, it seems likely that the Soviets wiped out much of the remaining population in the early 1960s. The western populations of the right whale in both oceans probably number only a few hundred animals, and in the North Atlantic there is high mortality from ship strikes and entanglement.

Although western Arctic bowhead whales appear to be making a strong recovery, bowhead populations both in the Okhotsk Sea and the eastern Arctic are small and highly vulnerable. The former was exploited illegally by the Soviets as late as the 1960s, and today probably numbers in the low hundreds. The eastern Arctic stock (which may well be at least three subpopulations which mix to an unknown degree) probably consists of several hundred whales. However, bowheads are now virtually gone from one of their historically most important habitats in this eastern range, the region of Spitsbergen Island and the Barents Sea.

Similarly, western gray whales, in sharp contrast to those of the California population, may number only 250 animals. The gray whale, which was still hunted by Korea as recently as the 1960s, now clings precariously to survival in its historic range off Japan, Korea and in the Okhotsk Sea. In the latter area, grays are threatened by oil and gas development in one of their principal summer feeding habitats off Sakhalin Island, although a joint U.S.-Russian scientific effort is monitoring this work.

With the exception of an apparently large and growing population off California, there is good reason to believe that all blue whale stocks are small and highly endangered. Reliable numbers do not exist on the size of the various blue whale populations around the world, but none appears to be very large, and we must sadly say that the future of this most magnificent of animals is still far from assured.

The Future

We do not have sufficient information to confidently assess the conservation status of many large whale populations, nor do we know whether complex issues such as pollution will create major problems somewhere down the road.

And now, like a recurring bad dream, whaling once again steps into the picture.

By the 1980s, the membership of the International Whaling Commission included many non-whaling nations as well as countries which, like Australia and New Zealand, had abandoned whaling and become strong advocates for whale protection. Swept along by these conservationist votes, the IWC finally passed a moratorium on whaling in 1986.

Since then, however, whaling has continued on a smaller scale. Much has been conducted under the guise of science, exploiting a provision in the convention that allows whaling nations to issue themselves permits to kill whales for research purposes. More recently, Norway has allotted itself a commercial quota which seems to increase every year.

The small minke whale, once derided by whalers as not worth the effort of killing, today bears the brunt of the industry's assault. While minke populations are probably large enough to withstand current catches, many environmentalists are concerned that this activity presages a major expansion of the fishery, complete with all the deception and lack of prudence that characterized the industry in the past. Indeed, we have already seen examples of this: genetic testing of whale meat on sale in Japanese markets has found many species other than those that are 'legally' hunted, including some that supposedly have protected status. Whatever happens, it is clear that any resumption of commercial whaling must be accompanied by watertight inspection practices, not only at sea but also at every stage on the path to the market.

But should whales be killed at all? I would argue that they should not be. There can be no doubt that human beings are inspired by the great whales. Anyone who has seen a humpback whale leap clear of the water in a full breach, or watched the unending immensity of a blue whale gliding past them underwater can understand this. I doubt that there are very many people who could witness such things and not be moved.

Whether we like it or not, not all species are equal. While the common cockroach is in its own way no less a miracle of evolution than the blue whale, the idea of using the cockroach as a focus with which to persuade people that the natural world is worth saving is untenable to say the least. But this *is* sometimes possible with whales.

Human beings have created some huge problems on this planet of ours, and only human beings can fix them. If we are to have any hope of doing this, we need to change attitudes, to somehow civilize ourselves with regard to the way that we view and value Nature. I believe that, if we make a commitment to not kill another whale, we will have taken a small but significant step towards this goal. I am under no illusions about the immensity of this task, particularly in the case of poor people in developing countries. Nonetheless, as Teddy Roosevelt understood well when he created the first national park, we have to start somewhere.

Human beings live by symbols. For a great many humans, whales have come to symbolize not only the reckless exploitation of the natural world, but the plight of the oceans and indeed of the planet itself. If we wish to preserve these things, whales are a pretty good place to start.

The most acrobatic of all whales, a humpback almost clears the surface in a spectacular breach off Hawaii. Whatever its function, the sheer exuberance of a breach — the single most powerful act in the animal kingdom — can inspire awe in even the most jaded of humans. No other animals have so moved our own kind, nor suffered so much at our hand, as the great whales.

In 1988, three gray whales trapped in ice in Alaska became the focus of worldwide attention as human rescuers attempted to free them. Two eventually escaped, but the third animal died. Ice entrapment is not an uncommon hazard for whales which feed in high-latitude waters, but most mortalities of this type go unobserved.

Although the rescue of the gray whales trapped in the Alaskan ice involved huge expense to reverse a common and natural event, it underscored the changing attitudes of humans towards whales. Although they are still sometimes hunted, whales have undeniably become a symbol for the plight of our small planet in the modern age.

The Classification of Cetaceans

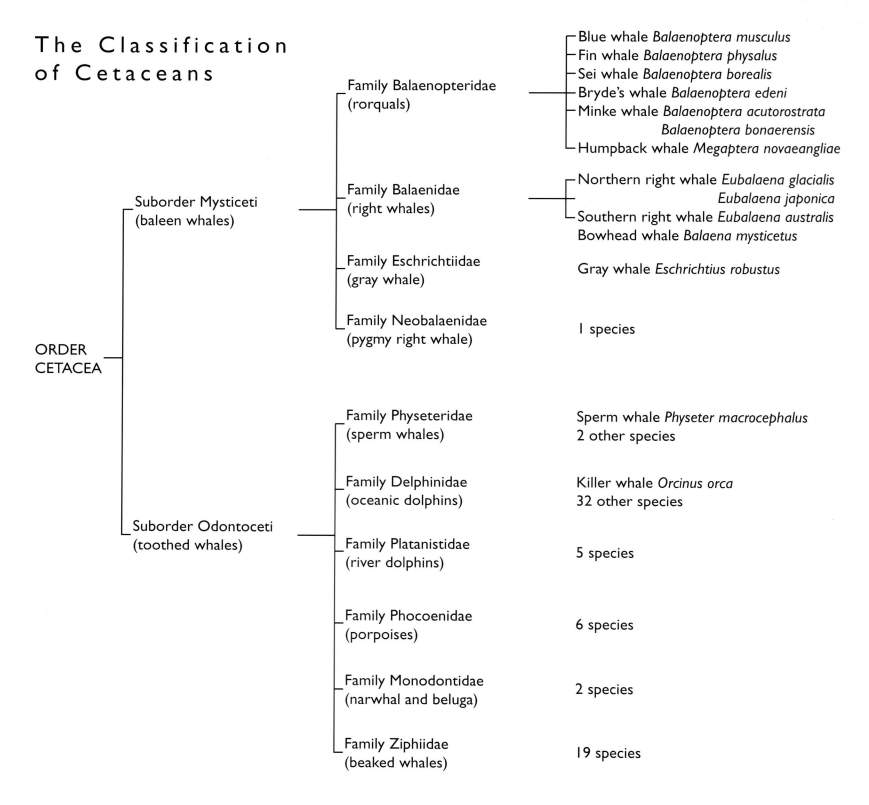

ORDER CETACEA

Suborder Mysticeti (baleen whales)

- **Family Balaenopteridae** (rorquals)
  - Blue whale *Balaenoptera musculus*
  - Fin whale *Balaenoptera physalus*
  - Sei whale *Balaenoptera borealis*
  - Bryde's whale *Balaenoptera edeni*
  - Minke whale *Balaenoptera acutorostrata*
    - *Balaenoptera bonaerensis*
  - Humpback whale *Megaptera novaeangliae*

- **Family Balaenidae** (right whales)
  - Northern right whale *Eubalaena glacialis*
    - *Eubalaena japonica*
  - Southern right whale *Eubalaena australis*
  - Bowhead whale *Balaena mysticetus*

- **Family Eschrichtiidae** (gray whale)
  - Gray whale *Eschrichtius robustus*

- **Family Neobalaenidae** (pygmy right whale)
  - 1 species

Suborder Odontoceti (toothed whales)

- **Family Physeteridae** (sperm whales)
  - Sperm whale *Physeter macrocephalus*
  - 2 other species

- **Family Delphinidae** (oceanic dolphins)
  - Killer whale *Orcinus orca*
  - 32 other species

- **Family Platanistidae** (river dolphins)
  - 5 species

- **Family Phocoenidae** (porpoises)
  - 6 species

- **Family Monodontidae** (narwhal and beluga)
  - 2 species

- **Family Ziphiidae** (beaked whales)
  - 19 species

Recommended Reading

It is a sobering thought that there are probably more books on whales today than there are right whales in the North Atlantic. Existing books on whales vary from outstanding to frankly pretty dreadful. Below are some of the best.

Whales and Dolphins by Anthony Martin and a team of experts, Salamander Books Ltd. London, 1990. A thoroughly researched and beautifully illustrated overview of cetaceans.

The Natural History of Whales and Dolphins by Peter Evans, Christopher Helm (Publishers) Ltd, London, 1987. An in-depth review of the biology of cetaceans.

The Sierra Club Handbook of Whales and Dolphins, by Steve Leatherwood and Randall R. Reeves, Sierra Club Books, San Francisco, 1983. Probably the best of the many currently available field guides to cetaceans.

Whales, by E. J. Slijper, Cornell University Press, Ithaca, New York, 1962. Although out of date in some respects, this remains one of the best and most thorough books ever written about the biology of whales, and is indispensable to the serious student of the subject.

In addition to the above, the WorldLife Library presents detailed looks at the biology and behavior of whales in the following books:

Beluga Whales by Tony Martin.
Blue Whales by John Calambokidis and Gretchen Steiger.
Gray Whales by Jim Darling.
Humpback Whales by Phil Clapham.
Killer Whales by Sara Heimlich and Jim Boran.
Minke Whales by Rus Hoelzel and Jonathan Stern.
Sperm Whales by Jonathan Gordon.

Finally, I would be remiss if I did not petition the reader to consider Herman Melville's classic, *Moby Dick*. Although stylistically it is unquestionably one of the messiest novels ever written, it contains a remarkably detailed account of the business of whaling as practiced in the 19th century, as well as some of the most glorious writing in all of English literature.

Biographical note

English by birth, Phil Clapham has lived in the United States since 1980. Recognized as one of the world's leading experts on large whales, he currently directs whale research at the Northeast Fisheries Science Center in Woods Hole, Massachusetts. He is also a Research Associate with the Smithsonian Institution in Washington DC, and a member of the Board of Governers of the Society for Marine Mammalogy. At one time or another, he has worked on most species of great whales, and has been an advisor on whale research and conservation to several governments. The author of sixty scientific papers and one other book (*Humpback Whales*, also published in the WorldLife Library series), he holds a Ph.D. in biology from the University of Aberdeen, Scotland.

Acknowledgments

No review of this kind would be possible without the contributions to knowledge of the scores of scientists who have worked to study whales, often in difficult conditions and sometimes over the course of entire careers – one of the perils of choosing a long-lived mammal as the object of one's research! I am particularly indebted to those men and women who have pursued long-term investigations of living whales, demonstrating as they have that much more can be learned from a live animal than from the countless carcasses provided last century by the whaling industry.

For their generous sharing of information and ideas, I am grateful to Bill Amos, Robin Baird, Bob Brownell, John Calambokidis, Sal Cerchio, Roxy Corbett, Jim Darling, Phil Hammond, Steve Katona, Scott Kraus, Finn Larsen, Christina Lockyer, Tony Martin, David Mattila, Stormy Mayo, Jim Mead, Per Palsbøll, Roger Payne, Charley Potter, Howard Rosenbaum, Karen Steuer, Jan Straley, Steve Swartz, Mason Weinrich, Hal Whitehead and the late Howard Winn. Many thanks to them all.